Glass

SIGNATURES

TRADEMARKS

and

TRADE NAMES

from the seventeenth to the twentieth century

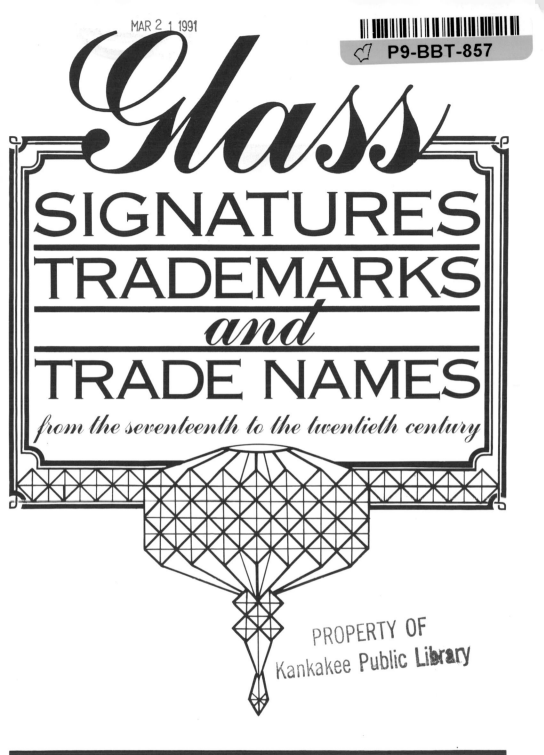

ANNE GEFFKEN PULLIN

Cover Design: Geri Wolfe Boesen
Interior Layout and
Cover Illustration: Anthony Jacobson

Library of Congress Catalog Card
Number 85-051345

ISBN 0-87069-462-6

10 9 8 7 6 5 4

Published by

Wallace-Homestead Book Company
201 King of Prussia Road
Radnor, Pennsylvania 19089

One of the ABC PUBLISHING abc *Companies*

Contents

Acknowledgments

Development of material into publishable form has been possible through help from many, particularly the staff at Corning's Library, the Fine Art and Interlibrary Loan Departments of the Orlando Public Library, glass manufacturers, dealers, authors, and friends.

I wish to express thanks to David Donaldson of the Morse Gallery of Art. His role as advisor for a paper for my Master of Art degree provided inspiration to organize this material for publication.

I extend special acknowledgment to my father for the education that he provided and to my mother whose love of antiques created an atmosphere in which I learned at a very early age bits about art and antiques; and, most of all, to my husband and children for their patience, understanding, and encouragement.

Introduction

How To Use This Book

An unorthodox method for alphabetizing has been adopted, because extensive use of unfamiliar foreign names created difficulties. To know if a word refers to a person, a city, or a manufactory is often difficult. Initials frequently blend with a last name to form a "new name." Umlauts and other foreign symbols alter a letter's alphabetical location making it difficult to combine different languages.

In hopes of facilitating use of this reference, all entries are listed in a simple "A, B, C" sequence, beginning with the first letter and taking each letter in order, disregarding the fact that it is an initial, a prefix such as Mc, or any other arrangement learned in school. For example, "B. Edwards" is found under "B" and appears before "Beilby Pintx."

The most prominent letter of a monogram is listed under the chapter for that letter. Monograms appear at the front of each chapter and are followed by alphabetical arrangements as explained above.

Because bottle marks are well recorded, most bottle marks are omitted, Trade names of commercial product manufacturers are included when they are similar to domestic or artware trade names or marks.

Unfortunately, marks are not actual size. A period after an initial may or may not be accurate due to inconsistencies in reference sources.

Few authors were as specific as Fauster whose references for the New England Glass Company detailed all punctuation. Important points for determining authenticity of a mark are a letter's style, proportion, size, and whether it is with serif or sans-serif.

When known, dates are given during which a mark was used. Available research material and time were too thin to obtain detailed data on numerous manufactories, such as when they were founded and when they ceased operation. Therefore, if a date is given as "1970s," it does not indicate that the manufactory was established or ceased operation during the decade, only that the mark was in use during that period.

An advanced connoisseur or student does not rely on signature alone. He instinctively analyzes each piece of glass. He may not require a written detailed analysis as outlined in the following questions. However, beginning students, general appraisers, and general antiques dealers will benefit by developing a flow chart with similar questions, especially for important items. Whether a glass object is signed or not, a written detailed analysis provides valuable reference material for completing an appraisal or for pursuing research at a future date when an item may no longer be available for inspection.

Sources of References

Inclusion in this book does not guarantee authenticity of a mark or signature, nor that the maker actually used the style mark to sign an item. Some references for this information are conflicting or non-available. Some sources are simply wrong, Many manufacturers used only paper labels. Therefore, be wary of assuming that a trademark is also used as a signature. On occasion, a signature may be a portion of a trademark.

This is intended to be a convenient and quick source for preliminary dating and identifying marked items and a guide for locating reference material. Not all entries listed were personally observed. Trade names, trademarks, and signatures were gleaned from many sources, some long since forgotten, for they were collected before formal research for a book began. Some trademarks and signatures were seen on appraised items or on glass at auctions and antiques shows. Numerous marks were referenced in book texts and illustration captions, and others were described in auction and exhibition catalogs. I am grateful to those authors whose research of a single subject provided the most complete information. An author's reference appearing at the end of an entry may be either the source of a mark or signature or a general reference for that entry.

Source materials did not always concur. Establishing dates for entries created many difficulties. Some references differed by one or two years, others by twenty or more. Occasionally an author referenced an impossible signature application method, such as "wheel etched," apparently having confused the etching process that requires acid with a wheel or needle engraving process. Should it be spelled "Kimball" or "Kimble?" Half the references use one spelling, half the other.

I submit this book to the publisher with mixed emotions of satisfaction and frustration. I am pleased that finally a quick-reference guide is available for marks that I encounter daily. I am frustrated with incomplete entries and possible errors. Hopefully, further research and constructive criticism from readers will allow correction of errors and fill existing voids, particularly for information on nineteenth century art glass. I would welcome receiving actual size, accurate tracings of any mark or signature that can replace less accurate drawings and verbal descriptions. In addition, I would like to secure information regarding unlisted makers' marks or artists' signatures active up to 1980.

How To Look at Glass

What could be easier than scratching a name and date on the bottom of a glass vessel? As previously stated, inclusion of a mark or a signature in this book does not guarantee authenticity. A signature only provides a clue for determining an object's origin. Its presence is not assurance that an object is "right," that is, by the named maker or of the date of its decorative style. For determining this, experience, study, and handling many different items are necessary. Nor does a mark's presence or absence determine an object's aesthetic quality. One acquires ability to determine this by study of fine examples and visits to museums.

In order to evaluate any object, a number of points should be specifically studied. Each detail is relative to a particular production or decorative technique, art movement, or artist. For example, presence of mold marks may or may not be correct. They are correct on an early pattern glass goblet but incorrect on a free-blown goblet. The following questions are intended as guides for developing expertise so that one does not rely on marks alone to determine origin and value.

When the significance of a question in the following analysis is not understood, further study of history or production methods is necessary. For example, a rippled surface appearance or undulations of an inner wall on a brilliant period cut glass bowl provides dating clues and indicates quality.

Research reveals answers to analysis questions and provides a valuable learning exercise. The experience, however, requires dedication, time, and often money in order to attend seminars or to purchase research material, both printed literature and study objects. These methods develop expertise and connoisseurship and facilitate intelligent use of material in this text.

Drawn with diamond point. Note the jagged edges of the very thin lines. Often used on works of contemporary glass artists. May be referred to as "incised" or "engraved."

Analysis Questions

What type material has been used?

Determining if lead has been used in making an item of clear glass is simple. Presence of lead causes an item made of clear glass to fluoresce bluish under ultraviolet light, while glass without lead generally fluoresces green-yellow or does not fluoresce at all. This method cannot be used for colored glass. However, scratches, tone, and heft are helpful points to observe for other type metals and for colored objects. Throughout glass history many formulas have been used. Although each type metal exhibits typical characteristics, distinguishing one from another becomes difficult, even for experienced glass specialists.

Other characteristics to observe

- What is the resonant quality of an item? When struck with the fingernail, does it have a deep ring, a ping, a thud?

- What is its relative weight to size when compared with examples of known metal and provenance? How thick or thin are the walls?

- When examined both in transmitted and reflected light, are impurities observed? If so, classify them. How refractive does the glass appear?

- What colors appear? How do hues vary? Are they yellowish, greenish, bluish, etc.? Are hues clear or muddy, intense or pale?

How was the object formed?

- Was it free-blown, mold blown, or a combination method?

- Do mold marks appear?

- Is there a pontil mark? How is it finished?

- Can tool marks be seen? For example, does one see tool scars about the foot, stem, or rim?

- Is the surface glossy or wrinkled? Does it display other visual characteristics?

- What are the tactile characteristics: silky, rough, heavy, light, thick, temperature?

- Are there undulations of an inner surface that are not perceptible at first sight?

- Are there striations within the glass?

- If bubbles are present, are they elongated, round, irregular? Do other occlusions exist?

- How have details like handles, stems, feet, etc., been applied and finished?

- Does the form have perfect symmetry; does it sag or appear out of round?

What type decorative treatment has been used?

- Is decoration within the glass, applied, or both?

- Does it appear to have been fixed by heat?

- What are its adhesion characteristics: flaking, peeling, rubbing, etc.

- Is there evidence of use of grinding tool, acid etching, sandblasting, or other surface treatment?

- Are colors opaque, semi-opaque, or transparent? How do tones compare with similar examples of the same period or by the same manufacturer?

- If painted, is there indication that a template or decal was used? Do design motifs repeat exactly or show variations?

- Do enamel colors appear to have been refired, showing a muddy tone or pitting?

- How has gilt decoration been applied? Does it appear to have been applied as a liquid or as gold leaf? What is its tone? Is it dull, glossy, thick, or thin?

Acid etched. Note the shadow and the soft outline of the letters. These can be very crude on forged signatures. Lines of authentic signatures on items of cut glass, for example, are generally very thin and clear. May also be referred to as "engraved," but this term is totally incorrect.

Made with a revolving burr of a Dremel. Note the rouletted line made when the head skips. Often used for forged Tiffany signatures and by contemporary glass artists on their works. May be referred to as "incised" or "engraved."

What is the decorative style, and at what period was this style adopted?

- What style is the decoration?

- Does decoration correspond to the body form that was popular during the period?

- Is any design element atypical of the supposed maker, period, or country of origin?

- Has a method of decoration or manufacture been used that was not in use or not developed until a later period?

Aesthetic valuation

- Is the item representative of a particular art movement?

- How does it compare, both technically and aesthetically, with other authentic works by this artist or manufactory? Is it superior or inferior to his customary standard? Does it have a counterpart, or is it unique?

- How does this item correspond to other contemporary artists' works? Is it better, as good as, or worse than others?

- Is the form well proportioned? Does the form suit the purpose?

- If decorated, is the design well balanced? Does it fit the form to which it is applied?

- Are colors harmonious and appropriate for the artistic period?

- Does the object have historic importance, either from provenance or because of historic position in glass technology, an art movement, or the creator's development?

- Does the analysis confirm the attribution of the signature?

Does evidence of usage, age or deterioration exist?

- Is crizzling present? Is the glass clouded or otherwise stained?

- Does the base show fine unpolished surface at contact points? Are they logically located or coarse and randomly placed?

- Is the glass body surface scratched? Do distress marks appear logical for age and purpose of object?

- Are chips or cracks (internal as well as external) evident? Are all parts intact?

Does the mark confirm the attribution?

- Are all design elements appropriate for the period when the maker was active?

- Is the method of manufacture in keeping with technical developments up to that time?

- Where is the mark or signature applied? What size is it?

- How is the mark applied? Is it molded, engraved, acid etched, painted, etc.?

- How neatly is it executed? Is it smeared, irregular, shaky, precise, etc.?

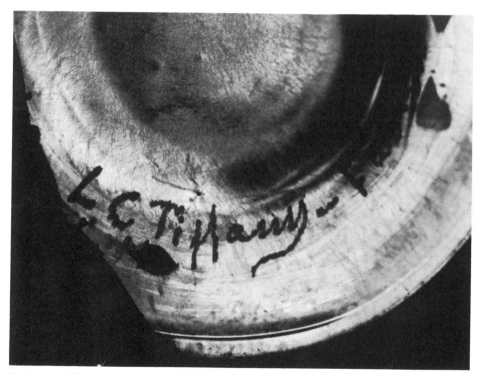

Authentic Tiffany signature. Note the uneven lines. These appear to be made with a vibrating instrument that is held in a steady direction of about 45 degrees from the perpendicular.

Symbols

Russian.

    Sig.: molded in bottom of "Russian" pattern pressed glass box

See Steuben.

    Sig.: white paper label with gold border, inked design number and price. Used 1905–1932.

Mr. Dupont, France. Retired worker at Baccarat, believed actively making paperweights up to 1930s. [Selman]

    Sig.: date cane of black, red, green, or blue on a white bar. The cane is usually in center of motif or close to bottom of pansies.

    1815–1830s

Peill and Putzler, Düren, Germany. Active 1960s. [Klessen/Mayr]

    Sig.: acid etched around mark on under side. Used on overlay glass with oxidized mottling.

Oertel & Co., design from the Haida trade school, Czechoslovakia circa 1913. [Neuwirth]

Shimada Glass Co., Osaka, Japan. Early 1900s. Lampshades. [Catalogue]

20th Century Manufacturing Co., N. Y., N. Y., circa 1900. Lighting devices. [Peterson]

20th CENTURY

See: Le Verrerie Francais or Charder.

   Sig.: candy cane embedded into glass

   Vase also inscribed with name of retailer.

OVINGTON/NEW YORK

Moses, Swan & McLewee Co., Trenton, N.J. Late 19th century, brilliant cut glass. Out of use by 1915. [Revi/JCK]

   Trademark

See: Leerdam. Artists' signatures.

   Copier:

   de Bazel:

   de Lorm:

   Lanooy:

See: J. & L. Lobmeyr.

Sig.: engraved or enamelled. Used after 1860. [Pazaurek]

M. J. Averbeck, Honesdale, Penna., 1892-1923. Retailer and mail order house for brilliant cut glass. [Revi]

Diamond Cut Glass Works, N.Y., N.Y. 1910-1917.

Diamond Glass Co., Royersford, Penna. Trademark active 1970s.

A. H. Heisey & Co., Newark, Ohio. Registered circa 1900. Pressed tablewares.

Sig.: Molded in glass.

See: Leerdam.

1919-1925, paper label:

1925-1928, paper label:

Since 1928, paper label:

Since 1970, molded:

Minneapolis Glass Co., Minneapolis, Minn.
C. 1800s, label for lighting ware. [Peterson]

Reported as forgery for Thomas Webb. Used
on Bristol, satin, etc. Etched or black
ink. [Cronin]

E. De La Chapelle & A. M. Paturle, Brooklyn, N. Y. Used after 1906 for blown lamp
chimneys. [Peterson]

Flemington Cut Glass Co., Flemington, N. J.
Brilliant cut glass. Later items, lightly
cut. Established in 1908, still operating
in 1964. [Boggess/Revi]

    Trademark: "--- CUT GLASS" within
    shield, encircled by "FLEMINGTON CUT
    GLASS CO./NEW JERSEY"

Schott & Gen. Late 1890s for various
wares. [Peterson]

    Sig.: etched

De Oude Horn Glassworks, Holland. In 1978, began making "Unica" wares. [Van der Meer]

 Sig.:

Ehrich & Grätz, Berlin, Germany. Circa 1880s, lighting wares. [Peterson]

 Sig.: impressed or etched

Paul Richter Co., Chicago, Ill. 1914-1940. Brilliant cut glass cutting shop.

 Trademark

United States Glass Co., Pittsburgh, Penna. Trademark. Made cut glass c. 1891-1910, and other production glasswares. See: monogram under "U."

The Dial Glass Works, Webb Shaw & Co., Stourbridge, England. Trademark registered 1901. [Manley]

Lötz Witwe, Austria, circa 1900. Art glass.

 Sig.: acid etched on base

Imperial Glass Co.   Commercial glass production.

   Sig.: Molded in pressed wares.

   1913:

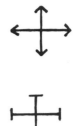

   1915:

L. Straus & Sons, N.Y., N.Y. Established
in 1888, active until at least 1915.
Brilliant cut glass. [Revi]

   Sig.: 3.5 mm. diameter, etched

Libbey.   Trademark registered circa 1902
for pressed cut glass blanks.   [Revi/
Fauster]

   Also believed to appear as a forgery on
   new wares.

William H. Lum, &
William H. Lum & Son, N.Y., N.Y.   Active
about 1915. Brilliant cut glass.

   Incorrectly printed in a reference.
   See: W. H. Lum.

Silver City Cut Glass Co., Meriden, Conn.
Established in 1905, still operating 1960s
or later. [JCK]

Val St. Lambert, Belgium. Trademark registered 1889. [Manley]

Krestalunie Maastricht, Holland. Trademark
used from 1925 to 1978. [Van der Meer]

Macbeth-Evans.   Assigned to Corning Glass
Works, Corning, N.Y.

   Trademark registered about 1880, etched
   or label. [AGR]

Viking Glass Co., Huntington, W. Va.
Active circa 1970s. [AGR]

Gill Brothers, Steubenville, Ohio. Early
1900s, for lighting wares. [Peterson]

   Sig.: etched or label

K. E. Jacobson & E. H. Fessenden, Brooklyn,
N. Y. C. 1800s lighting wares. [Peterson]

Dukes Ltd., Platts Works, Stourbridge,
England. Glass manufacturer. Trademark
registered 1910. [Manley]

Josephenenhütte, Gräfe, Schaffgotsch'sche
Glasfabrik in Schrieberhau/Riesengeberge,
Germany. [Wittenau]

   Signature found on a Biedermeier beaker.
   [Pazaurek]

Gill Bros, Steubenville, Ohio. Circa
1900s, trademark for lighting wares.
[Peterson]

C. & S. Bishop & Co., Lancashire, England.
Glass manufacturers. [Manley]

   Trademark registered 1883

   Trademark registered 1905

George Borgfeldt & Co., N.Y., N.Y. Jobber, active circa 1915. Brilliant cut glass. Trademark. [Revi/JCK]

Derby Crown Glass Co., Derby Crown Glass Works, Derby, England. Glass manufacturers. Trademark registered 1916.

Ottawa Cut Glass Co., Ottawa, Ontario, Canada. Brilliant cut glass. Trademark. [Revi]

Crown Crystal (attributed to), Australia. C. 1930s. [Graham]

   Sig. molded on tumbler decorated with acid etched florals.

Outline of the Australian continent

Ouseburn Glass Works, Newcastle-on-Tyne, England. Glass manufacturers. Trademarks registered 1894.

George Drake Cut Glass Co., Corning, N.Y. 1899-1908. [Ferrar/JCK]

Thornhill Lees, John Kilner, Yorkshire, England. Glass manufacturer c. 1792–1857. [Manley]

Isaac Jacobs, Bristol, England. Trademark registered 1805. [Manley]

Oscar O. Friedlaender, N.Y., N. Y. Circa 1890s. "Fireproof" or "Indifferent" used with lion at later periods. Lighting wares. [Peterson]

Stykes & Macvay & Co., Albion Glass Works, Yorkshire, England. Glass manufacturers. Trademark in use from about 1863. [Manley]

Smith Brothers. Operated decorating studio for Mount Washington Glass; later opened their own business in 1876. [Revi/Padgett]

   Sig.: printed in red on base of painted opal wares

Wapping Glass House, England. C. 1680s. No specimen recorded, but records report the mark impressed on a seal.

Lion and coronet

Henry Greener & Co., Sunderland, England. Late 19th century. Lacy pressed (1870s-1880s), slag, etc. Mark used from 1884. [Manley/Will s]

    Sig.: Molded in pressed ware.

1928   after 1928

George Davidson & Co., Eng. Established in 1867, quality pressed, slag, and other domestic wares. Reproducing old lines of 1880s. [Manley]

    Sig.: Molded in ware.

William Meyerstein & Co., London. Retailer of large selection of glasswares. Trademark registered 1882.

John B. Higbee, Bridgeville, Penna. C. 1907-1916. [Innes]

    Sig: Molded on a glass spoon and other domestic wares.

    Said to be reproduced at this time.

North British Glass Works, John Moncrieff, Perthshire, England.   Trademark in use from 1872. [Manley]

Josef Pelikan (1828-1920), Baden-Baden & Haida. [Weiss]

Pelican in a landscape

George Ravenscroft (1632-83), England. Perfected lead glass formula. Mark used from 1677. [Newman/McKearin]

   Sig.: impressed on a seal about 1/2-inch diameter.

Sowerby & Neville (1855-72), Sowerby & Co. (1872-81), Sowerby's Ellison Glassworks (1881-on), Gateshead-on-Tyne, Eng. Inexpensive pressed glass, slag, spangled, etc. Marked from 1876 on. [Manley/Will s]

   Sig.: molded in ware, usually under base, sometimes in interior. May also have registry mark.

F. Steüben & Co., Erfurt, Germany, 1890s, lighting wares. Trademark. [Peterson]

Alfred Lippert, London, England. Trade name active circa 1886. [Schack]

    Sig.: molded in pressed slag glass with British registry number

Henry Brooks & Co., Glass manufacturer, London and Melbourne, Australia. Trademark used from 1875. [Manley]

Strathearn Glass Co., Crieff, Scotland. 20th century makers of paperweights and other glasswares. [Manley]

    Trademark registered about 1964

    Molded in base of paperweight

Henry Birks & Sons, Montreal and other Canadian cities. See: House of Birks. Trademark active 1915, listed as jobber of cut glass. [JCK]

Demer Bros. Co. Inc., Great Bend, Penna. Cut glass. Trademark active circa 1915. [JCK]

Mount Washington Glass Co., New Bedford, Mass., established in 1837. Made Albertine and Crown Milano wares, glossy finish with heavy gilt or floral decoration. [Padgett]

Sig.: in red, fired on underpart of object

occasionally with numbers, and/or "C M"

T. B. Clark & Co. (1884-1930), Honesdale, Penna. Cut glass. [Boggess/Revi]

References regarding location and marks of these firms are confused.

Attributed to Maple City Glass Co.:

Regarded only as a trademark, not used as a signature, discontinued by 1915:

Landgrafe Karl of Hesse-Cassel, Germany. Franz Gondelach (1663-1726) in 1688 became court engraver. Biblical, allegorical, historical, & pastoral subjects in hochschnitt and intaglio of Baroque style. Succeeded by Johann Heinrich Gondelach (1663-1723). [Newman]

Sig.: workshop mark engraved on base   8-point rosette

Friedrich Winter (d. 1712), Silesia. Engraved rock crystal style Baroque subjects. Set up first water-powered mill for glass engraving. [Weiss]

Workshop mark. Fir tree

A. H. Heisey & Co., Newark, Ohio. Registered c. 1908 for domestic wares. [Peterson]

Schneider: Le Verrerie Francais, established 1913, France. Art Deco style cameo wares. [Arwas]

Sig.: diamond point on foot or side

Schott & Gen., Germany. Circa 1905, used for lamp chimneys and scientific wares. [Peterson]

Keystone Cut Glass Co. Ltd., Hawley, Penna. Succeeded by Geo. W. Murphy. 1902-1918. [JCK/Revi]

Buckley-Newhall Co., N. Y. Circa 1910, used for lighting wares. [Peterson]

See: Steuben. [Gardner]

Acid etched or label on brilliant cut and art glass.

Stevens & Williams, England. 19th century makers of art glass. [Grover/Gardner/ Beard]

Sig.: in cameo on acid cut-back vase, at bottom.

Weiss & Biheller Ltd., London, England. Circa 1906, trademark molded or label for domestic wares. [Peterson]

Key Glass Works, London, England. Glass manufacturers. Trademark registered 1909. [Manley]

Franklin Flint Glass Works (1860) and Gillinder & Sons (1867-71), Philadelphia, Penna. Label used on chimneys. [Belknap]

Whitefriars Glass Works, London. Established in 1680. Since 1848, made paperweights; also produced cut glass. Resumed name in 1962. Sold to Caithness in 1981. [Selman]

    Sig.: paperweights, signature cane. Still used by Caithness.

    Diamond point on side of paperweight

    Salesman's sample paperweights marked "Proof" and with design number in diamond point on bottom.

Hamon Handcrafted Glass, Dunbar, W. Va. Active 1970s.

E. Pickett & Co., Leeds, Eng. Active early 20th ca., still active 1965. Brilliant cut glass, painted and fired plate glass for windows. Trademark. [DBG]

Ratcliff Glasshouse (attributed to), Southwark, London, Eng. Late 17th or early 18th century. [Will.s]

Female figure shooting a bow

Moritz Kirchberger, N.Y., N.Y. C. 1900,
lighting wares. [Peterson]

A. F. Pears, London, England.   Glass
manufacturers.   Trademark used from about
1890. [Manley]

Samuel Clarke (active 1860s to about 1892),
London. Candlemaker. Patented design for
night lights. [Newman]

    Sig.: molded in base of Fairy lamp.

    Trademark in use from about 1862

Wolf & Gross, N.Y., N.Y. C. 1893, tableware. Label or enamel. [Peterson]

See: Perthshire. Paperweights. [Selman]

    Date letters in canes from 1969 to 1983   "A" through "O"

J. Mortlock & Co., London, England.
Trademark registered 1880. [Manley]

Anchor Hocking Glass Corp., Lancaster,
Ohio. Tablewares.

   Sig.: molded in glass

Vereinigten Lausitzer Glaswerks, Weiss-
wasser. [Wittenau]

Index of Signatures, Trademarks, and Trade Names

A

Attributed to Akro Agate, USA.   Twentieth
century depression glass.   [Florence]

    Sig.: molded

Not identified.   Probably Europe, c. 1910.
[Hilschenz]

    Enamel on foot rim of vase in white
    enamel.

Direktor Adolfa Beckerta, art director at
Loetz, 1909-26.   Steinschönau Trade School
for Glass, c. 1911-19, Czechoslovakia.
Iridescent and other art glass.
[Neuwirth/ Pazaurek]

    Sig.: c. 1920, etched

Arnold Eiselt, Czechoslovakia.   Engraver.
1907-14 instructor at Haida trade school.
[Pazaurek]

"KK FS ST" & a number

30

August Helzel, Meistersdorf. Glass engraver. See: "AH" & "AHM." [Pazaurek]

Adolf Rasche, Haida [Bohemia]. Engraver at
Haida trade school late 19th or early 20th
century. [Pazaurek]

Anton Kothgasser (1769-1851) Vienna. Miniaturist painter. Worked on glass from
1812-30. Many imitators. See: "Anton
Kothgasser." [Weiss]

    Sig.: used on enamel beaker.   "A K" in monog.

Arthur Löwenthal, (d. 1879), Berlin, Germany. Engraver of figural subjects.
[Pazaurek]

William Allen Cut Glass Co., Johnston,
Penna. William Allen, president. Fine
quality cut glass during the Brilliant
Period. [Farrar]

    Sig.: diamond point, used circa 1905-09   A

    1909-1913, an oval white label with red
border

Allen Cut Glass Company, 1913-20. See:
William Allen Cut Glass Co. [Farrar]   **A**

Akro-Agate Co., Akron, Ohio. Established in 1911 as jobbers for marbles. From 1932 to 1948 made decorative domestic wares from opaque colored glass. [Florence]

    Sig.: molded

T. J. Collet Cut Glass Co., Johnston, Penna. 1921-22, successors to Allen Cut Glass Co. [Farrar]

    Sig.: diamond point   A

Mr. Anderson. Early 1900s, lampshade painter at Handel. See: "Handel." [Grant]

    Sig.: painted or scratched on shade.   A.

August Böhm (1812-90), Meistersdorf. Traveled in England and America. Engraver in Biedermeier style, chiefly figural subjects. [Weiss]   A BOHM

Alfredo Barbini (b. 1912). Murano glass designer. Since 1950, has operated own studio. Devised technique "a masello", sculpturing a solid glass mass without moulding or blowing. [Newman]   A. BARBINI / MURANO / 1970

A. Brugnon, c. 1880s, probably France. Enamel decoration on champagne glass. [Exhibition]   A. BRUGNON

Arthur Cunette, early 20th ca. Lampshade
painter at Handel. See: "Handel." [Grant]

AL

Louis C. Tiffany. See Tiffany. Pieces
from his private collection.

    Sig.: diamond point

A-Col

Fostoria Glass Specialty Co., Fostoria,
Ohio, c 1908. Used for lighting wares.
[Peterson]

ACORN

Albert Louis Dammouse (1848-1926), France.
In 1818, began making vessels of porcelain
paste and glass mixture, similar to pâte de
verre. "S" represents "Sèvres" where he
was a potter. [Arwas]

    Sig.: molded in base

A D

Adam Renneisen, working 1675, Nuremberg,
Germany. Engraver. [Weiss]

ADAM RENNEISEN

A. David. Sculptor at Baccarat for sulphides in paperweights. Working 1963.
[Auction]

    Signed on sulphide.

A DAVID 63

Andries Dirk Copier (b. 1901), Holland.
Associated with Leerdam Unica Studio
1914-67. Extended production of houseware
to include individual ornamental designs.
See Leerdam and Copier monogram, under "L."
[Van der Meer]

A Dopier
1924

Amédée Duc de Caranza, France. 1890-1918
associated with H. A. Copillet et Cie,
Noyon, France. Designer of art glass,
including iridescent and cameo. See: Duc
A. de Caranza. [Arwas]

Sig.: in cameo on side near base of
iridescent cameo vase.

9. de CARANZA

Stenciled acid etched:

A. de CARANZA.

May also include signature of H.
Copillet.

A. DE CARANZA/
H. COPILLET OISE 1588
NOYON

André Delatte, Nancy. In 1921, founded
small glass works to produce cameo pieces.
[Arwas]

Sig.: in cameo on side of vessel

DELATTE
Nancy

or

lightly stencil-etched polished signature against a matt ground.

DELATTE
NANCY

Other variations exist.

A. Douglas Nash Company. Used before 1928. See: "Nash." [Messanelle]

Sig: on experimental gold iridescent vase. Number refers to size, letter to color.

A.D.N.A. X13

J. Seaton & Co., Glasgow, Scotland. Maker of decorated glass wares. Trademark registered 1895. [Manley]

★AEROLITE

Aerozon. Not further identified. [Blount/Auction]

Sig.: in cameo near base of floral cameo design on muffineer with silver mounts bearing German Reich's marks in use since 1888.

Edward A. Power & Co., Pittsburgh, Penna. Late 1890s, trademark for tablewares, pressed or blown. [Peterson]

A. F. à Schüramnn (1730-83), Amsterdam. Engraver in stipple with hatching and diamond point. Dated pieces from 1757 to 1780. [Weiss]

A. F. à SCHURMANN
SCULPSIT ANNO 1771

Alfred Finot (1876-1947), France. Designer for A. Walter. Sculptor and member of Société des Artistes Français, exhibited with them in 1935 [Benezit/Arwas]

AFinot

Afors Glassworks, Sweden. Part of the AB Afors group. Established 1876 by master glass workers from Kosta. Boda and Kosta are members of the group. Still in business.

AFORS

Andreas Friedrich Sang, Weimar, Germany. Working 1719-60. Some works are dated. [Weiss]

A. F. SANG

A. Gibion, c. 1914. Not further identified. [Auction]

Sig.: enamel on base of enamel decorated ewer.

A GIBION / 1914/244

See: Aug. Heiligenstein.

Sig.:

On painted panel

A. H. Unidentified painter. Circa 1911. See: Mohn.

Sig.: beaker with enameled view of Dresden, Germany.

A. H. / S. MOHN

Kerr Glass Mfg. Corp., Los Angeles, Calif. Trademark active 1976. [AGR]

August Helzel (b. 1851), Meistersdorf. Engraver at fachschule. Student and son-in-law of Franz Zahn. [Pazaurek]

Sig.: engraved.

Andreas Vincenz Mattoni (1779–1864), Carlsbad, Czechoslovakia. Founder of school of
engravers at Carlsbad, Bohemia. Teacher of
Ludwig Moser. [Weiss]

A. H. MATTONI

Not identified. Used on a milk glass vase
painted with romantic children. French,
last quarter of 19th century. [Auction]

Signed in enamel.

AHNE

Also bears the seal: "Republique Fran-
çais/Exposition Internationale de 1878 &
Weltausstellung/ in Wien 1872" and
another mark.

Anton Heinrich Pfeiffer (1801–1866), Carlsbad, Bohemia.   Follower   of   Mattoni.
[Weiss]

A. H. P.

Compagnia Venezia & Murano, circa 1880s,
Venice, Italy.

Used on bowl of cobalt and white glass
with portrait of Admiral Pietro Loredan
(d. 1439). [Schack]

AHP

André Hunebelle, working 1920s, France.
Molded ware, slightly frosted in Art Deco
style or semi-opaque Cubistic influence.
[Arwas]

Sig.: molded vase and signature.
Sometimes with "France."

A. HUNEBELLE
FRANCE

Molded vase with brown wash.

MOD DEP DE A HUNEBELLE/
R COGNEVILLE/FRANCE

Auguste Jean, working 1878-1900. Potter &
glassmaker, early worked with iridescent
glass with engraved or enamel decoration.
Late work, free form. [Arwas/Klesse]

Sig.: gilt script on base in polished
pontil.

AJean

AJean

A. J. Hall Company, U.S.A. Formerly
decorator at Handel. Operated own glass
decorating shop for lamps c. 1899-1928.
[Revi]

Sig.: molded in glass.

A. J. HALL CO.

A. J. Imberton. Decorator working in Paris
circa 1886. Signed near bottom with
enamels on leaded panels decorated in
Japanese taste. [Auction]
Possibly misread: see J. P. Imberton

A. J. IMBERTON / PARIS

A. J. IMBERTON / 1886

See: "Anton Kothgasser."

A K

Arthur Kohn, Birmingham, England. Glass
manufacturer. Trademark registered 1908.
[Manley]

Akro-Agate Co., Akron, Ohio. Established
1911 as jobbers for marbles. From 1932 to
1948 made decorative domestic wares from
opaque colored glass. Dissolved in 1951.
[Florence]

Sig.: Label

Alphonse Lechevrel, England. Working 1877.
Cameo worker at Hodgetts Richardson and at
Webb. [Beard/Grover]

    Sig.:

A L 1877

A L 1877 / GEO. WOODALL
sometimes w/title

Vincent Works, William Thomas Sugg, Westminster, England. Trade name registered
1875. [Manley]

ALBATRINE

Albert Wiegel (1869-1943), Kassel, Germany.
Engraved portraits on plaques after photo-
graphs. C. 1900, executed some work in Art
Nouveau; after 1905, carved figures from
solid glass blocks. [Newman]

    Sig.: engraved on plaque of Queen
    Victoria.

ALBERT WIEGEL

Alexander Seifferd (1660-1714), Arnstadt.
[Weiss]

ALEXANDER SEIFFERD 1705

.C. G. Alford & Co., N.Y., N.Y. Jobbers
circa 1872 to 1918. Brilliant cut glass.
[Revi/JCK]

Alfredo Barbini (b. 1911). Barbini Glassworks, Murano, Italy. Opened his own
furnace in 1950. Block sculptures.

    Sig.: engraved on sculpture.

ALFREDO BARBINI / MURANO
1970

    Paper label:

Al Gesù, factory in Murano, Italy. First recorded in 1537, operated until late 18th century. Made opaque white glass with polychrome decoration. [Newman]

AL GESÙ

Almy & Thomas, Corning, N.Y. Cutting shop for rich-cut glass 1903-1907. [Farrar]

    Sig.: acid stamped

Alois Wudy (b. 1941), Germany. Master glass painter. In 1965, became head of glass painting department at Zwiesel Fachschule.

ALOIS WUDY 1969

Alphonse Morel, Lodelinsart, Belgium. Active c. 1876. Glass maker. [Manley]

Allen & Moore, London. Active 1851. Paperweights. [Cloak]

A & M / LONDON 1851

New England Glass Works, trade name for reactive ware shaded from ruby to amber at base. Label. [Fauster]

Mount Washington/Pairpoint. Heavy textured
glass. Painted on inside. [Padgett]

Ambrosius Egermann, Bohemia. [Weiss]

    Sig.: enameled beaker.

Adolph Mocho, Sr., Vineland, New Jersey.
Active 1960s. Signed on paperweight.
[Cloak]

A. MOCHO

Johann August Mohn (b. 1800), Dresden.
Known for fine painting. [Weiss]

    Sig.:

A MOHN fect. 1817

Silver & Flemmings, Albert Marius Silver,
London. Glass manufacturer and retailer.
Trademark registered 1880. [Manley]

Attributed to a forger. See: "Nash."
[Cronin]

    Sig.: engraved script on art glass

A. NASH / TIFFANY FURNACES

Anchor Hocking Glass Corp., Lancaster,
Ohio. Tablewares. "Fire King" is trade
name for oven ware.

    Sig.: molded in glass.

Gill Brothers Co., Steubenville, Ohio. Circa 1901, trademark for lighting wares. Etched or printed label. [Peterson]

FINE
ANCO
FLINT

André. Cameo vase. Possibly French. [Blount]

AnDRE

André Thuret (1898-1965), France. Glass sculptures, crystal overlay. [Polak/Bröhan]

    Sig.: engraved

andré thuret

Andries Melort (1779-1849), Dordrecht & The Hague. Engraved flat glass in diamond point with scenes from Dutch paintings. [Weiss]

ANDIRES MELORT

Andrieu. See: Montcenis. [Jokelson]

    Sig.: on sulphide

ANDRIEU F

Angelo Barovier (b. 1927). Son of Ercole Barovier. Manager of Barovier & Toso. [Newman/Polak]

Angelo Barovier Murano 60

Angelo Barovier 1971

Seguso Vetri d' Arte. Angelo Seguso, Ware designed by Flavio Poli, Italian 20th century . [Newman]

ANGELO SEGUSO

Stuart & Sons, Stourbridge, England.
Tradename registered 1889. [Manley]

ANTHEMON

Anthoni Wilhelm Mäuerl (1672–1737), Nuremberg/London.   Engraved "Laub- und Bandelwerk" designs. [Weiss]

ANTHONI WILH. MÄUERL

Anton Kothgasser, Vienna.   Active 1820.
Miniaturist. [Weiss]

   Sig.:   enameled   beaker,   occasionally
added date and address.

ANTON KOTHGASSER /
IN WIEN 1822

Albert Parlow. Early 20th century, American.   Lamp shade painter at Pairpoint,
later at Handel.

   Sig.: painted on lamp globe.

A. Parlow

Bermondsey Glass Works, 1900, London.
[Manley]

   Sig.:

APPLIED ART

A. R.   Unknown. Signed on enameled beaker,
probably Vienna, c. 1830. [Exhibition]

A R

Notsjö Glassworks, Nuutajärvi, Finland.
Established 1793. Chiefly maker of tableware, some art glass. [Newman]

   Trade name used since 1971.

ARABIA

Dagobert Peche (1889-1923). 1917-18, designed for Wiener Werkstätte. Designer for Loetz Witwe. [Pazaurek/Arwas]

    Sig.: c. 1912, in gilt script on underside of vessel

Seguso Vetri d'Arte, glassworks at Murano, Italy. Since 1934, producing art glass.

    Sig.: engraved on vase with gold inclusions, engraved signature. Circa 1950. Association not confirmed.

ARCHIMEDE SEGUSO MURANO

Architect Arnold Nechansky (1888-1938), Austria. Designer for Loetz and Haida Trade School. [Arwas]

ARCH.NECHANSKY
Loetz

British Petroleum uses this shield with "BP" as a trademark. Association not confirmed.

    Sig.: molded on dinner plate and other domestic wares.

ARCOROC, FRANCE

Alphonse Georges Reyen, France. In 1877, worked with Rousseau. 1890s, opened his own shop, decorated items in cameo and cased glass. [Arwas]

    Sig.: incised script. Sometimes dated and "Paris."

a. Reyen

G Reyen

Gabriel Argy-Rousseau.   See: G. Argy-
Rousseau.

ARGY ROUSSEAU

Anna Roemers-Visscher (1583-1651), Amsterdam. Decorator of calligraphic motifs in
diamond point. [Weiss]

ROEMERS

St. Louis Glass Works, France.   Standard
export quality cameo works, c. 1900 to
1914. [Arwas]

Art.   Signed in cameo on cameo vase.
Attributed to France, c. 1900. [Blount]

Martha Eliza Norris, Middlesex.   Trademark
registered 1888. [Manley]

ART GLITTER

GLASS

Art Verrier, St. Louis, France. Used about
1920-25 on tortoise-shell glass. [Klesse]

Sig.: diamond point under foot

A. Rub.   Attributed to Europe, c. 1900.
[Neuwirth]

Signed in gold under the base of color-
less cased glass with threading inlay,
etched, and gilt.

Aert Schouman (1720-1792), The Hague/
Amsterdam. Stipple engraved ware. [Weiss]

A. SCHOUMAN FEC - 1752

ASG Industries, Kingsport, Tenn. Trademark
active circa 1976. [AGR]

J. A. Sious (?).   Attributed to Russia,
circa 1910. Cameo vase. [Ptocku]

    Sig.: incised

Duryea & Potter, N. Y., N. Y. Circa 1901,
trade name for decorative glass. [Peter-
son]

ATHOSGLASS

Hazel-Atlas Glass Co., Wheeling, W. Va.
Circa 1902, domestic wares.

    Sig.: molded.

ATLAS

Aubin.   Three-dimensional hunting scenes,
England,   first   half   of   19th   century.
[Newman]

AUBIN

Audubon Crystal Ltd.   West Port, Conn.
Limited edition plates, c. 1978. [Kovel]

Believed to be signed

Augusté Claude Heiligenstein (b. 1891), France. Some works executed at Pantin and at Monte Joye signed with their trademark. Also, designed independently and for others. [Arwas]

Sig.: in diamond point, sometimes w/ number, date, or title, usually on base. Used on enamel decorated vessel.

AUG. HEILIGENSTEIN

Aureliano Toso, designer active 1960s at Barovier & Toso. [Auction]

AURELIANO TOSO 1968

Steuben Glass Works. Tradename for iridescent art glass developed by Frederick Carder. Registered circa 1903-04. [Gardner]

Sig.: engraved on bottom. Also accompanied by letter and numbers, may also be used on paper label.

Stamped in white enamel or acid etched for items made for Haviland & Co, circa 1910-1915.

AURENE
HAVILAND & CO.

Macbeth-Evans Glass Co., or their predecessor. Etched on lamp chimneys, c. 1890s. [Peterson/Catalogue]

AURORA

Ase Voss Schrader. Active 1950s.

Sig.: diamond point on important pieces.

AVS ⚓ 1959

See: Loetz. "Austria" used after 1891 for export pieces.

A. Verlys, France. After 1930. Molded decorative frosted glass items, influenced by Lalique. Heisey acquired the license to produce wares from the molds from 1935 to 1951.

Sig.: molded and engraved on ware made in France. American made pieces are diamond point signed, without "France" and "A." However, some references state that the American product was identified with a label only.

Avitra Corp., N.Y., N.Y. Trademark for gift wares, active c. 1970s-80s, perhaps earlier. [G & T]

Sig.: acid etched.

Trademark

AVITRA

HAND MADE
AVITRA
CRYSTAL

Alice Woodall, England. Daughter of George Woodall; worked at Webb in cameo. [Beard]

A W

Almeric Walter (1859-1942), France. School of Nancy. Circa 1908-15, worked at Daum. Opened own workshop with Henry Bergé for Pâte de Verre about 1919. After 1919, designer's name appears on superior designs. [Arwas]

Sig.: molded on pâte de verre.

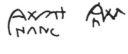

Designer's name may be inscribed:

Alfred Finot

E. Royer

Henri Bergé

AW / N / B

AW / N / HB

Jean-Bernard Descomps (1872-1948), France. Sculptor and painter. [Benezit]

JEAN DESCOMPS

M. Corrette

CORRETTE S.C.

A. Houillon

Mercier

MERCIER

J. Cayette

J. CAYETTE

J. CAYETTE SC

L. Jan

L. JAN

American Wholesale Corp., Baltimore Bargain
House, Baltimore, Md.   Mail order distributor of brilliant cut glass and other wares,
c. 1922-?. [Revi]

Rick Ayotte, American.   Since 1976, paperweights of bird subjects. [Selman]

AYOTTE w/ number &
year

Adam Zumbach, Zurich, Switzerland.   Working
1671-88.   Stained glass roundels and battle
scenes. [Gessert]

B

Jan Boekhorst, Haarlem, Netherlands. Glass engraver and painter. [Gessert]

Jacob Pieter van der Bosch (1868-1948), Holland. Active about 1893 to 1920 in the Art Nouveau movement. [Van der Meer]

    Signed on a stemware service produced about 1906

Edgar Benna (b. 1899), Breslau. Glass engraver. [Weiss]

Baccarat. Paperweights. [Selman/Cloak/Newman]

    Early period "B" in cane by one of two men named Battestine.

    Signature/date cane

Ray & Robert Banford, USA. Started work in 1971. Lampwork in paperweights. [Selman]

    Sig.: in red, white, & blue cane for Bob; different colors for Ray.

B

Dominik Biemann. Engraved glassware. Many other signature forms; refer to index.

J. D. Bergen Co., Meriden, Conn. Glass cutters of brilliant period designs. Active about 1885 to 1922. Used blanks made by Pairpoint. [Revi]

Sig.: acid etched

Boda Glass Works, Sweden, c. late 20th century, member of the Afors Group. [Newman]

Sig.: etched on foot of stemware.

Beyer & Co. GmbH, Neustadt/Waldnaab, Germany. Active 20th century, producing drinkware. [Körting]

Boyd's Crystal Art Glass, Cambridge, Ohio. Bernard C. Boyd (b. 1908) purchased Degenhart factory. Produced hand pressed animals, figures, etc.

Sig. molded on side.

Baccarat, Muerthe, France. Most important French contemporary maker of crystal. Founded 1764. Wide variety of products.

Trademark registered 1860 and still in use, label or acid etched.

Etched on perfume atomizers.

Cane of paperweight made to commemorate visit of Marshal Francois Canrobert to the factory.

Circa 1965, used with trademark on 66 paperweights to commemorate bicentennial. Etched. [Selman]

Also numbered in diamond point as follows:

26 millefiori   "A" TO "Z"

20 filagree paperweights   "1" to "20"

20 couronne weights   "21" to "40"

Revival of sulphide paperweights in   Sculptor's name, date,
1953. Signed on edge of bust.   & subject

Contemporary limited edition paper-   Signature cane,
weights   date & number

Engraved on cameo ware, circa 1915   BACCARAT
                                       1915

Bakewell Glass Co., Pittsburgh, Pa., 1808 to 1882. See index for Bakewell, Pears & Co. [McKearin/Innes]

Moulded on window pane. c. 1830-45.

BAKEWELL

Molded on drawer pull, c. 1825-35. Used on other pressed items.

BAKEWELL & ANDERSON/
PITTSBURGH

Balboa, Italy. Trademark, active late 20th century Venetian glass. [G & T]

American Wholesale Corp. Baltimore Bargain House, Baltimore, Md. Trade name registered 1890. Mail-order business for cut & ornamental glass, tableware, etc. [Peterson]

BALTIMORE BARGAIN
HOUSE

Frederick W. Buning, N.Y., N.Y. Lighting wares, trademark registered 1893. American importer for unidentified Austrian maker. [Peterson]

Bar or Barz. Engraved signature on commercial quality cameo vase, late 19th or early 20th century, attributed to France. [Venzmer]

Signed:

John Jenkins & Son, London. Glass retailer. Trademark registered 1935. [Manley]

Sig.: molded in vase

BAROLAC

George Davidson & Co., Ltd., England. Trade name active 1975, for pressed lead crystal glassware. [EGD]

BARONET

Barovier & Toso, Murano, Italy, 1936 to present. Angelo Barovier (b. 1927), director and glass sculptor. [Newman]

 Sig.: inscribed on vase

BAROVIER & TOSO/
MURANO

Ariel Bar-Tal (b. 1920, Budapest), Israel. Sculptures and vessels. Designer and glass worker, used Pyrex as material for works. [Grover]

Barthmann KG, Dorotheenhütte, Wolfach/ Schwarzwald, Germany. Active late 20th century. Domestic wares. [Körting]

Cristallerie de Champagne Verrerie/ Bayel. France. 1666 to present. Table & art lines; limited edition plates since 1977. [G & T/Kovel]

 Trademark

 Sig.: etched on base

BAYEL

Bibi & Co., N.Y., N.Y. Table & gift ware. Trademark active 1970s. [G & T]

Bartlett-Collins, Co., Sapula, Okla. Trademark active 1970s.

B. & Co., Ltd., England, late 19th century. [Manley]

Sig.: used on a bowl the design of which is attributed to John Northwood

B & CO LTD

Charles T. DeForest, N.Y., N.Y. Decorative items. Trade name registered 1884. [Peterson]

Etched or printed

BEAUMIROIR

Beauté. Czechoslovakia, probably early 1900s. [Blount]

Sig.: Engraved on lamp base.

Beauté

G. R.(?) Becken. Art Deco vase w/enamel decoration. [Auction]

Sig.: enamel on side

Becken

Henry Bedigie, USA. Lampshade painter at Handel. [Grant]

Sig.: painted or scratched on reverse painted shade w/landscape subject

Bedigie

Long Bridge Glass-House, Belfast, Ireland, c. 1771-1826. Established by Benjamin Edwards. [Will s]

    Sig.: molded raised letters on bottom of tall tapered decanters with fluting about base, 2 neck rings, & disk stoppers.

                               B. EDWARDS BELFAST

William (1740) & Mary Beilby (1749-97), Newcastle-upon-Tyne, England. Decorators. [Newman/Weiss]

    Sig.: white or colored enamels on drinking glasses.

                               BEILBY JUNR, PRINTXIT
                               AND INVT N'CASTLE 1762

                               BEILBY PINTX

    Used before 1765   W. BEIBLY, JUNR.

Carl V. Helmschmied, active 1904-34. [Revi]

    Sig.: molded   BELLE WARE C V H

Bendor. Not further identified. Seen on commercial quality cameo vase and on vase with enameled design. [Auction]

    Sig.: cameo. Also seen in enamel.   *Bendor*

Benedikt von Poschinger, Oberzwieselau.
Established in 1906, produced designs after
Georg Carl Reichenbach. [Schrack]

Trademark

Monogram of Georg Carl von Reichenbach

Bengt. Began as designer in 1953 at Skruf
Glass Works, Edenfalk, Sweden.

BENGT EDENFALK SKRUF

Benny Motzfeldt (b. 1901), Norway. About
1954, started working with glass. During
1970s, design director for Plus Organiza-
tion, export designs. Sculptural vases.
[Grover]

Sig.: "Norway" may be added to signature.

Henri Bergé. Designer at A. Walter,
France. Active 19th century. [Arwas]

J. D. Bergen Co., Meriden, Conn. Cut
glass: manufacturer, designer, & cutter of
fine wares. Used Pairpoint blanks. Active
c. 1885 to 1922. [Boggess/Revi]

Trademark etched

Etched script:

Kaiser, Alboth, Germany. Limited edition engraved goblets, Famous Composers Series, c. 1972. [Kovel]

BERLIN

William Joseph Bernstein, N. Carolina. Sculptures.

    Sig.: usually dated.

Klaus Bertelsmann (b. 1924), Germany. Decorator at Glashütte Süssmuth from 1968 to 1970s. Maker of heavy cylindrical vessels. Developed glass engraving technique while an illustrator for Die Zeit, in Hamburg. [Klesse]

BERTELSMANN SCULPT

Gill Bros. Co., Steubenville, Ohio. Lighting wares. Trademark registered c. 1885. [Peterson]

    Etched or printed label

    Etched or printed label, c. 1890

    Etched on lamp chimney, no date. [Meadows]

BEST SAXONY CRYSTAL

Abraham & Strauss, Inc., Brooklyn, N.Y. Trademark registered 1925, used on paper label. Retailer of cut glass and table wares. [Revi]

Beyer & Co. GmbH, Germany. Active late
20th century.

    Sig.: etched on foot of lead crystal
stemware.

BEYER

Attributed to Bradley and Hubbard, U. S. A.
Early 20th century. Makers of leaded
shades in the style of Tiffany and other
art metal wares.

    Sig.: metal disk applied to underside
of metal lamp base with leaded shade

See: Dominik Bieman

BI

Bob Biniarz, California. Independent designer, late 20th century. [Grover]

House of Birks, Montreal, Canada. Established by Henry Birks and active as retailers, 1879 to present. [Boggess]

Sloan Glass Inc., Culloden, W. Va. Trademark active 1970s. [AGR]

Jules Paul Brateau (1844-1923), France.
After 1903, designed in pâte de verre.
[Hilschenz/Arwas]

    Signed on side with gold foil

B. K. Co. Unknown. USA. Molded in fruit
knife, probably early 20th century.

B K CO

Blenko Glass Co., Milton, W. Va. Established by Wm. J. Blenko, active 1855-1933.
Early period: stained glass church windows;
since 1929, decorative and commercial ware.
Still in business. [G&T]

    Trademark

BLENKO HANDCRAFT

Buckley-Newhall Co., N.Y., N.Y. Lamps &
accessories. Active 1910. [Peterson]

BLUE RIBBON

Boda Glass Works, Sweden. Member of the
Afors group. Circa 1970 s, managed by
Erik Rosen. Table and art ware. [Grover]

Erik Höglund

Boda 379·1265 "m. Högluhd"

    Sig.: Bertil Vallien (b. 1938), Sweden.
Designer. Signed with diamond point

BODA-AFORS UNIK/
929 B VALLIEN 1970

Boers, B. Worked in diamond point, 18th
ca., Netherlands. [Weiss]

Signed work known

Philip Boileau, glass painter active 1907. Painted on Wave Crest Ware. [Grimmer]

Signed work known

Bonnet. Brilliant period cut glass. Not further identified. Probably early 20th century, USA or Canada. [Boggess]

Boris Dudchenko, Greensburg, Penna., active late 20th century. Free-form sculptures.

Boris Dudchenko

J. W. Bartlett, N.Y., N.Y. Lighting wares. Trademark registered in 1870s. [Peterson]

BOULEVARD

Bakewell, Pears & Co., Pittsburgh, Pa. Pressed wares. [Innes/McKearin]

    Signed on an item made of patented process of double layer glass fused by pressing.

B P & CO PAT'D
SEPT 29, 1874

C. H. v. Boselager Netherlands. 18th century, worked in diamond point. [Weiss]

Signed work known.

Big Pine Key Glass Works, Big Pine Key, Fla. Trademark active 1970's. [AGR]

Bradegaard, Sweden.   Gift & tableware.
Trademark active c. 1970s.

Bradley & Hubbard Mfg. Co., Meriden, Conn.
Makers of leaded shades and other art metal
items such as desk sets.   Trademark active
circa 1915. [JCK]

    Label on art metal/leaded glass lamp
    shades.

Braggie, Henry, USA.   Lampshade decorator
at Handel Lamp Co.   Early 20th century.
[Grant]

Braggi

Bricht (or Bright).   See: Baccarat.
c. 1824. [Cloak]

    Sig.: sulphide doorknobs & drawer pulls.

BRICHT

Keith Murray, New Zealand architect, working at Stevens & Williams, Brierley Hill
Glass   Works,   Stourbridge,   England,
c. 1930s.   Tablewares.   [Stevens   &
Williams]

    Sig.: acid etched on base

Keith Murray
S BRIERLEY

See: Stevens & Williams.

Trade name etched on cover of lead
crystal jar, 20th century.

Etched in yellow under base of vase,
c. 1928.
Trademark registered in 1926. (Manley)
Royal Warrant received in 1919.

Lewis P. Dexter, N.Y., N.Y. Lighting
wares. Trade name active 1904. [Peterson]

BRIGHTSTAR

Pilkington Bros., Ltd., St. Helens, Eng.
Changed to Pilkington Glass Mfg. Co., Eng.
& Canada. Trade mark registered 1877.
Decorative and domestic wares. Trademark
printed or molded. [DBG]

James Hateley, Birmingham, England. Glass
manufacturers. Trademark registered 1887.
[Manley]

Philippe-Joseph Brocard, France. Active
from 1867, died 1896. Produced 13th & 14th
century Syrian-style decoration. Brocard
et Fils (1884-1896). [Arwas/Polak]

Sig.: gilt script on base of enameled
vase.

BROCARD/PARIS/1876

Gilt script

Brock Glass Co. Ltd., Santa Ana, Calif. Trademark active 1970s. Table and gift wares. [G&T]

Broma. Unknown. Possibly early 1900s, France. [Ptocku]

　　Signed on a cameo vase.

Broma

Benjamin R. Watson (active 1921-42), Corning, N. Y. Cut & engraved ware. [Farrar]

　　Sig.: on best pieces, worked into design or incised on bottom.

B. R. W.

Robert Bryden, active 1976-78. Maker of paperweights. [Kovel]

Signed work known

Bernard Schagemann (b. 1933), Germany Since 1959 designer of industrial art glass. In 1964, began teaching at Zwiesel.

　　Sig.: "Zwiesel" or "F. S." may be added to signature.

B SCHAGEMANN 1969

Burgun & Schverer & Co., Verrerie d'Art de Lorraine, France. Presently known as Verrerie de Meisenthal. Established 1711, began production of art designs in 1855 under Désiré Christian. Acid & wheel engraved work. [Arwas/Taub]

　　Sig.: etched and gilt trademark on base in several variations:

BS&Cº

*VERRERIE D'ART
DE LORRAINE
BS & Cº*

Andenken
Glashütte
Meisenthal 1902

Boston & Sandwich Glass Co., Sandwich, Mass., 1825–88. [McKearin]

B S & CO

    Molded in base of salt dish, c. 1830s or 40s.

B & S GLASS CO.

    Forgery, acid etched, not typical of the factory's productions. [Cronin]

B & S G CO

Burley & Tyrrell Co., Chicago, Ill., Active 1870–1920. Wholesalers of cut glass. [JCK/Revi]

    Trademark

Ferdinand von Poschinger (1815-1867), Germany. Buchenau Glassworks, Bavaria. Worked in Art Nouveau style c. 1890s. [Arwas/Hilschenz]

Trademark circa 1900

Sig.: gilt letters on base. May also add model numbers: "Ferd. von Poschinger Buchenau Bayern Glashüttenwerke"

"Ferd. von Poschinger Buchenau Bayern Glashüttenwerke No. ---" Consecutively numbered from "40" to 840," circa 1900 to 1906

The Glass Batch Supply Co., London. Glass manufacturer. Trademark registered 1891. [Manley]

BUNYIP

See: Clarke. Trademark registered 1884 for Pyramid & Fairy Lamps. [Manley/Peterson]

BURGLARS' HORROR

August Otto Ernst von den Busch (1704-1779), Hildesheim, Germany. Worked in diamond point accented w/black pigment, floral & pastoral subject on goblets. [Weiss]

BUSCH FECIT 1744

See: BRW (Benjamin R. Watson). Cut and
engraved ware. [Farrar]

B. W.

B. W.   Unknown.   Attributed to Germany
circa 1900-1910. [Neuwirth]

   Sig.: etched relief on a cameo vase

C

G. H. Vischer, Switzerland. Active 1580–1605. Stained glass painter. [Gessert]

Not identified. Brilliant cut glass, circa 1900, possibly American. [Boggess]

Not identified. Twentieth century American.

    Molded in bottom of amber color pressed bucket, 2" tall.

Glassworks of Carl Goldberg, Haida, Bohemia. See: Goldberg. [Arwas]

Kristallfabrik Theresienthal Niederbayern (Lower Bavarian Glass Works), established 1834. [Jugendstil]

    Monogram of designer: Hans Christiansen (1866–1945), on side of goblet.

Ed Euypers, Holland. Active 1925; designer at Maastricht. [Van der Meer]

Raffinerie (refinery) Conrath & Liebsch, Steinschönau, Bohemia. Late 19th or early 20th century. In business in 1906. Worked with Professor Beckerta. [Pazaurek]

Crystal Import Corp., N.Y., N.Y. Trademark active 1970's. [G & T]

Crown Milano ware. See: Mount Washington Glass Co., Trademark registered 1892. May appear with a number.

Sig.: acid stamped black ink

Some forgeries also reported to be applied with black ink. Crown may be omitted; CM may appear within a lozenge.

Cambridge Glass Co., Cambridge, Ohio,. 1901-1954, reopened briefly, closed 1954. Inexpensive domestic and art ware. Pressed wares.

Molded. Used after 1920.

Clichy Glassworks at Clichy-la-Garenne, France. Produced paperweights from 1846-57. [Cloak/Selman]

Sig.: in cane of paperweight with red, blue, green or black initial cut into strawberry diamond motif on base of paperweight.

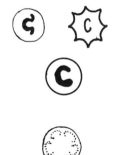

C-scroll garlands of millefiori.

Consumers Glass Co., Montreal, Canada. Trademark active 1970's. [AGR]

Lauensteinerhütte, 1701-1870. "C" represents Calenberg, the district where the glass was made. [Weiss]

    Sig.: on covered vase, cobalt color w/cut & gilt design.

A lion rampant with "C"

Caithness Glass, Ltd., Scotland. Established 1960. Paperweights by Paul Ysart. [Selman/Cloak]

    Sig.: on base in diamond point script.

CAITHNESS 1963

    Diamond point on base.

CAITHNESS, SCOTLAND with edition number

    Etched block letters.

CAITHNESS

Giovanni Calandrelli (wk. 1832, d. 1852). Rome/Berlin/Dresden. Engraver. [Weiss]

CALANDRELLI

Steuben Glass Works, Corning, N.Y. Calcite, a white ware used for lamp shades, developed by F. Carder. Trademark registered c. 1915. [Gardner]

    Sig.: etched in low relief, may appear as part of the design.

Not identified. Floral design painted with
a dull cream enamel on a commercial quality
vase to simulate cameo work. [Auction]

Sig.: acid stamp block letters each in a
square shield w/clipped corners.

CAMEO

Canadian system for dating containers.
[Stevens]

Molded in wares on bottom.

1940 Jan.-Mar.	.
Apr.-Jun.	..
Jul.-Sep.	...
Oct.-Dec.	....
1941 Jan.-Mar.	.⎯
Apr.-Jun.	..⎯
Jul.-Sep.	...⎯
Oct.-Dec.	....⎯

Another line added for each 1942 & 1943.

Canton Glass Co., Hartford City, Indiana
trademark active 1970s. [AGR]

Carbone Glass Co. Division of Pairpoint.
[Padgett]

Trademark

Carl Banks, worker at Pairpoint Mfg. Co.
Used after 1910. [Newman]

Sig.: engraved on base of paperweight.

CARL BANKS

Carl Moritz von Scheidt (active 1816), painter of fine quality views of German cities. Signature may also appear with that of "Mohn," and be dated. Used other variations of signature. [Weiss]

CARL MORITZ VON SCHEIDT

Carlo Moretti. Used on a facet cut vase, c. 1950's. [Auction]

    Sig.: engraved.

CARLO MORETTI

Carl Schappel, Haida, Bohemia. Paper label used on engraved stemware, c. 1914.

Donald Carlson, Pacifica, Calif. Designer. Received M.A. in 1972 from San Francisco State College. [Grover]

Carl V. Helmschmied (active 1904-34), designer and decorator of opal glass wares. C. 1890s worked for C. F. Monroe. [Revi]

CARL V. HELMSCHMIED

Carolyn Mollie Smith, USA. Active 1970s to 1980s. Maker of paperweights. [Selman]

    Sig.: diamond point on base.

Carpé. Two layer cameo vase of commercial quality. [Auction]

    Sig.: cameo script on side near base.

CARPÉ

    On the bottom of same vase, in acid stamped block letters

CZECHOSLOVAKIA

Caspar Gottlieb Langer (active 1749), Warmbrunn/Silesia. Engraver. [Weiss]

CASPAR GOTTLIEB LANGER IN WARMBRUNN GLASSCHNEIDER 1749

Caspar Creutzburg (active 1689), Gotha/ Amsterdam. Diamond point engraver.

 Sig.: diamond point on goblet. May be with or without date.

CASP. CREUTZBURG
FECIT. AM 19 JULY 1689

Castle Cut Crystal, Italy. Trademark active 1970's. Table and gift ware. [G & T]

Édouard Cazaux, France. Designer for Gueron. C. 1920s–30s. [Arwas]

 Sig.: moulded in pâte de verre.

Cynthia Bryden, USA. Decorator at Pairpoint c. 1970s. [Padgett]

 Sig.: painted on decorated vase.

Corning Cut Glass Co., Corning, N.Y. 1901–1911. Late mark. [Farrar]

 Sig.: acid stamped

"C C G" in an oval

See Dorflinger. Paper labels. Both styles reported to be forgeries supposedly used by Dorflinger's son to verify his father's productions. [Cronin]

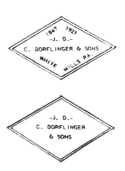

C. Durand. Lampshade with reverse painted seascape, America, 1920s. [Auction]

C. DURAND

Celta. Intaglio signature on Art Deco vase with acid cut and enamel decoration. Not further indentified. [Auction]

CELTA

T. G. Cook & Co., Philadelphia, Pa. Registered 1873. Used for pressed, cut, or blown glass tableware. [Peterson]

CENTENNIAL

Century Inkstand Co., N.Y., N.Y. Trademark registered 1893. [Peterson]

Ceraglass Co., Inc., Hackensack, N.J. Table and gift wares. Trademark active 1970s. [G & T]

Attributed to Johann Kunckel, Potsdam. Circa 1630(?)–1703. [Weiss]

   Sig.: used on a silver mounted ruby glass punch pot.

C. F.

Charles F. A. Hinrichs, N.Y., N.Y. Trademark registered 1872. Label on lighting wares. [Peterson]

C. Fauré, Limoges, France. Circa 1925.

   Sig.: gilt letters on an enameled vase.

C. FAURÉ/LIMOGES

Gérard Duffraisseix, after 1901, successor to Charles Field Haviland.

Listed by Peterson as stamped on table and decorative wares. Doubtful if used on glassware.

C F H
G D M

C. F. Monroe Co., Meriden, Conn.

Sig.: stamped on metal mounts of "Wavecrest," "Nakara," and "Kelva" glass

C. F. M.

Reported to be a forgery used on decorated and undecorated opal ware that was made at that period to resemble Monroe's products, signed on glass [Cronin]

C. F. M. CO.

Camer Glass Co. Inc., N.Y., N.Y. Table and gift wares. Trademark active 1970s. [G & T]

Gundy-Clapperton & Sons, Ltd. Active 1905. Maker of brilliant cut glass. [Stevens]

C. Géri... Art glass vase with encased powdered glass. Probably Europe, pre-1900, Nancy school. [Venzmer]

Signed with black enamel.

Corning Glass Works, Corning, N.Y. Used from about 1929. [Gardner]

Sig: acid stamped

Chandler Specialty Mfg. Co., Boston, Mass.
Trademark registered 1902. Label on lighting wares. [Peterson]

CHANDOE.

Chapelle, Nancy, France. Used on glass
base of lamp. [Auction]

    Sig: impressed into glass.

CHAPELLE/NANCY

Le Verre Français. Charder, combined from
the names Charles and Schneider.

    Sig.: generally in cameo on the side and
used with "Le Verre Français," engraved
on the foot or bottom of vessels,
c. 1926 to 1933. On later pieces, occasionally both names are engraved in
diamond point. [Schack/Arwas]

Charder

Le Verre Français

Engraved, used c. 1930-33

Charder

Name of retailer stenciled on base of
vase c. 1925

STEWART ET C.
NEW YORK / FRANCE

Charles Catteau, born in Douai, 20th century. Painter of landscapes, member Society of Artists, & Salon d'Automme.
[Benezit]

    Sig.: incised design on overlaid and
carved vase, c. 1925.

CH. CATTEAU

Charles Champigneulle (1853-1905), Paris,
France.   Glass painter; studied with his
father in Metz.   Executed works for Hotel
du Figaro and other buildings.

    Art Deco design verre Eglomisé panels
designed by Jean Dupas and executed by
Champigneulle c. 1934. Date of attribution possibly incorrect.   Signed with
silvered block letters. [Auction]

CH CHAMPIGNEVILLE FECIT
PARIS

Charles Herbert Thompson, Stourbridge, England.   Glass manufacturer.   Trademark
registered 1901. [Manley]

George Davidson & Co. Ltd., England. Domestic and decorative wares.   Trade name
act., 1960s. [BGD]

CHIPPENDALE

Jefferson Glass Co., Follansbee, W. Va.
Trademark active 1907. Domestic and decorative wares. Label. [Peterson]

CHIPPENDALE

Choko, John.   Millville glass worker.
Makes large limited edition paperweights.
Active c. 1974. [Kovel]

Believed to be
signed

Chouvenin.   Attributed to France, c. 1900.
Used on cameo and enameled vase. [Blount]

    Signed in enamel.

Joris Johannes Christian Lebeau (1878-1945). Designer at Leerdam. From 1926 to 1929 worked in Bohemia making individual art wares. [Van der Meer]

Sig.: diamond point

Chris- Lebeau - Febr - 1927-
UNICAAT - MOSER - FECIT
TCHECOSLOVAQUIE - 1038.

Cristallerie et Verrerie de Vianne, Boulogne-sur-Seine, France. Trade name active 1970s.

CHRISTIANA

Christian Gobrecht, 1785-1855, died in Philadelphia, Pa. Engraver and medalist, known for portraits of Washington and Franklin. [Innes]

Sig.: used on sulphide on a tumbler, attributed to Bakewell, Page, & Bakewell, Pittsburgh, c. 1826.

CHRISTIAN GOBRECHT

Christian Klepsch (b. 1943), Germany. [Schack]

Sig.: diamond point

Christian Klyssch 73

François Christian (1874-1906). Christian Frères et Fils, etc. after 1896. See: D. Christian. François was the brother of Désiré. Some authors attribute this signature only to items designed by François, others to Désiré. [Blount]

Sig.: cameo

Christian Meisenthal
I.

engraved

Christoph Dorsch (1676–1732), Nuremberg, Germany. Diamond point engraving on covered pokal. [Weiss]

CHRISTOPH. DORSCH FECIT. ANNO 1712 DEN 23, ABRIL

CHRISTOPH DORSCH FECIT ANNO 1712

J. F. Christy, Lambeth, England. Mid-19th century decorator of opal vessels. [Wakefield]

Signed work known

Ciriama. Attributed to French school. Two-layer cameo vase. [Blount]

C. J. Meier, 18th c., Netherlands, engraver in diamond point. [Weiss]

Signed work known

Clyne Farquharson, England. Worked at John Walsh and at Stevens & Williams c. 1930s. [Polak]

    Sig.: etched.

Carl Koepping (b. 1848). Designer, worked with Friedrich Zitzmann. [Arwas]

    Sig.: on base, used on colored Art Nouveau crystal from 1896 to 1900

C. Koster. 18th c., Netherlands, engraver in diamond point. [Weiss]

Signed work known

Christoph Labhardt (b. Switz., d. 1695). Swiss engraver in hochschnitt and tief-schnitt working in Silesia. [Polak]

Sig: on plate with wheel engraving and diamond point details.

C. LABHARDT FECIT 1689

Clairay Glassworks, c. 1950s. Made glass that was thick walled and internally bub-bled and marbled with decorations by Au-guste Heiligenstein. [Arwas]

Signed.:

CLAIRISTAL

T. B. Clark & Co., Honesdale, Pa. Cutting shop for brilliant cut glass and gilt decorating. Active 1886 to 1930. [Revi/Boggess]

Discontinued by 1915. Believed to have been used only as trademark, not for signing wares.

Active in 1915. Etched.

Clark

Possible forgeries of these exist in versions of the circle with bottle, script "Clark" with or without "Trade Mark," and a block letter version. Note for oversize and uneven edges of mark, and new glass.

Clarke's Pyramid and Fairy Light Co. Ltd., England. Trademark registered 1891. [Manley/Peterson]

    Sig.: molded in lamps, label on lamp oil bottles.

Clayton Mayer & Co. Ltd, England. Domestic glassware trademark active 1960s. Trade name. [BGD]

CLAYMER

Caspar Lehmann (1570-1622), Prague/Munich. Reputed to be first to use wheel engraving c. 1590-1605. [Polak]

    Sig.: beaker with wheel engraved decoration on Venetian "cristallo" glass.

C. LEMAN F. 1605

Clichy Glass Works, France. Established 1837. Paperweights. [Selman]

    Sig.: in cane. May also be a fragment of name.

CLICHY

Macbeth-Evans Glass Co., Pittsburgh, Pa. Trademark registered 1884. [Catalog]

    Etched on lamp chimney.

Arthur Lazenby Liberty, London, England. Listed by Manley as "oriental warehouse-men." Trademark registered 1888.

CLUTHA

James Couper & Sons, Scotland. Art glass
vase designed by Christian Dresser
(1834-1904). "Clutha" glass, patented
circa 1880s, is embedded with air bubbles
and aventurine. [Arwas]

    Sig.: acid etched on base

Charles Mulvaney & Co., active 1785-1835,
Dublin, Ireland. Glass decanter, lamps,
girandoles, etc. [Davis]

    Sig.: moulded in base of decanter.   C M & CO

C. M. Hoffmeister. Enameled Beaker, 19th
century Biedermeier, attributed to Bohemia.   C. M. HOFFMEISTER PINTX
[Auction)]

Carl Moritz von Scheidt, active 1816,   C: MO: V. SCHEIDT PIN.
Dresden/Berlin. Fine painter of city   BERLIN 1816
views. [Weiss]

Corrine Nobert, USA. Lampshade painter,
early 20th century at Handel. See: Handel   **CN**
[Grant]

Corning Glass Works, Corning, N. Y.
Trademark registered 1909, molded or
label. Tablewares. [Peterson]

Faulkner Bronze Co., Birmingham, England.
Trademark registered 1901. [Manley]

Cohansey Glass Mfg. Co., Bridgeton, N.J.
Established 1870 for windows, flasks and
holloware. [McKearin/Peterson]

    Trade name   COHANSEY

Coleman Lamp Co., Wichita, Kansas. Trademark registered c. 1913. Lamps. [Peter-
son]

**Coleman
Quick-Lite**

Collectors' Weekly, an antiques publica-
tion, Kermit, Texas. Limited edition   Believed to be signed
plates of cobalt glass, introduced 1971.
Made by Big Pine Key Glass Works, Fla.
[Kovel]

Col. Luciano Ferro. Used on art glass vase
with inlay.

    Sig.: engraved on bottom.   COL. LUCIANO FERRO 1953

C. Dorflinger & Sons, White Mills, Pa.
Trademark registered c. 1892. Believed to   COLONIAL
have been used on colored art glass,
c. 1916-1921, as well as brilliant cut
glass. [McKearin/Peterson]

Aristidé-Michel Colotte (1885- 1959). Settled in Nancy c. 1920. Vases, deeply cut w/matt and polished surfaces. [Arwas]

Sig.: diamond point, some etched, some marked "Piéce Unique."

Clayton Mayer & Co. Ltd., Britain. Trade name for decorated tableware. Active 1960s. [BGD]

COLOURCRAFT

Oneida Community, Ltd., Oneida, N.Y. Oneida Community of Perfectionists, founded c. 1847 by John Humphrey Noyes. Shared worldly goods, practiced group marriages. Trademark registered 1914, domestic glass wares, silver, etc. [Peterson]
Probably only used as a label.

COMMUNITY

Conlow-Dorworth Co., Palmyra, N.J. Jobbers for cut glass. Active about 1915-1920. [Revi]

Copillet et Cie, (1895-1900), Noyon, France. Art glass. [Klesse-Mayr]

Sig: in pontil with muffel color

Smith Brothers decorating shop, New Bedford, Mass. Worked in the decorating shop of the Mt. Washington Glass Co. until 1871, when they opened their own decorating shop. [Fauster]

> Sig.: On a "Burmese" vase with painting of the "Santa Maria"

COPYRIGHT BY
A. E. SMITH

> Plate sold by Libbey at 1893 Columbian Exposition and also marked with printed red circular Libbey mark.

COPYRIGHT 1893 BY
A. E. SMITH

Flygsfors, Sweden. Mark of the factory engraved on the bottom or printed on a label, active 1950s. Art goods. [Auction]

COQUILLE FLYGSFORS

Cork Glass Co., Ireland, c. 1783-1818, used on decanters. [Wills]

> Sig.: molded in base with block letters.

CORK GLASS CO.

Corning Cut Glass Co., Corning, N.Y. Established 1901, closed 1911. Not a part of the Corning Glass Works. [Farrar]

> Sig.: acid stamp on brilliant cut glass used during early period.

CORNING CUT GLASS CO.

A. Douglas Nash Co., Corona, N.Y. Successor to Tiffany Studios. Operated from 1928 to 1931.

> Sig: on base of earliest pieces, c. 1928.

CORONA

86

Will & Baumer Co., Syracuse, N. Y. C. 1900, label for lighting wares. [Peterson]

Corona Cut Glass Co., Toledo, Ohio. Trademark registered c. 1906. Label on cut and engraved ware. [Revi]

Correia, Santa Monica, Calif. Contemporary art glass studio established c. 1960s by Steven V. Correia. Lamps, vessels, etc.

   Sig.: diamond point in base

CORREIA

St. Louis Glass Co., France. Commemorative sulphide paperweight for coronation of Elizabeth II of England. [Auction]

   Sig: stamped on base.

COURONNEMENT 2-6-53

Cowie Bros., Glasgow, Scotland. Trademark registered 1889. [Manley]

Nazeing Glass Works Ltd., England. Trade name for mouth blown stemware and tumblers. Active 1960s. [BGD]

CRAFTSMAN

Cristalleries d'Albret, Vainne, Fr. Since 1966, sulphide paperweights, regular or overlay editions. Since 1972, Limited edition plates. Gilbert Poillerat, designer. [Selman]

Sig.: acid etched on base.

Also signed on edge of bust w/name of subject, date sculpture made, and initials of artist.

Creative World. Stained glass, limited edition plates, c. 1972.

Believed to be signed

Macbeth-Evans, Pittsburgh, Pa. Established late 19th century. First quality lime glass lamp chimneys. [Auction/Catalog]

Sig.: etched on top of chimney with reference to proper Rochester burner to be used with this chimney design.

CRESCENT

NO 2
ROCHESTER

Clarke's-Pyramid & Fairy Light Co. Ltd., London, Eng. Later version of Fairy Lite. Shade of clear uncut glass with peg base that fit the candle nozzle of dining table chandeliers and candelabra. Trademark registered 1894. [Manley/Newman]

CRICKLITE

Crider. Paperweight maker, USA, 20th century.

Sig.: engraved on base

Crider
1978

Cristallerie de Champagne, Verrerie Bayel. Table and art objects. Trade name active 1970s. [ANV]

CRISTAL DU BARROIS

Etablissements Jerome et Bonnefoy et Cie, Paris. Art glass, goblets and tablewares, trade name active c. 1970s. [ANV]

CRISTAL ILLE-DE-FRANCE, VERISSIMO

Cristallerie d'Art. France. Moved to Pantin c. 1855. Became Stumpf, Touvier, Violette, c. 1900. Height of artistic production c. 1880-1900. After WWI merged w/ Legras et Cie and operated as Verrerie et Cristallerie de St. Denis et Pantin Réunies. [Arwas]

Sig.: engraved on base of cameo vase. Same vase also with title and monogram on the side.

Used after 1900. Seen engraved on two-layer cameo vase.

See Gallé. After 1889, an industrial line
of cameo glass was produced by using acid
baths. This line was in addition to the
Art Line of individual designs that were
hand worked. [Block/Garner]

"Modelle et decor déposé" means model and
decoration are registered or patented designs.

Paper labels:

Cristallerie Lorraine, Lemberg (Moselle), France. Handmade tableware and decorative items. Trade name active 1970s. [ANV]

CRISTALLERIE LORRAINE

Cristallerie Schneider, Lorris, France. Active 1970s. Ornamental objects, vases and art glass. See: Schneider. [ANV]

CRISTALLERIE SCHNEIDER

See: Muller Frères, Croismare. Circa early 1900's, Nancy school.

Sig.: engraved on two layer cameo vase

Signed in cameo on cameo vase

Henri Cros (1840-1907), France. Researcher at Sèvres Porcelain Works, revived pâte de verre. [Arwas]

CROS

William Richard Pullen, London. Glass mosaic and stained glass maker. Tradename registered in 1889. [Manley]

CRYGLAMOS

Crown Crystal Glass Có. Ltd., Sidney, Australia. C. 1930s. Pressed wares. [Graham]

Paper label of crown outline

CROWN CRYSTAL/
GLASS CO. LTD./SIDNEY/
MADE IN AUSTRALIA
Reg._____

Crown Cut Glass Co. Inc., Hancock, N. Y.
In operation by 1903. Trademark active
1915. Cutting shop for Brilliant Period
cut glass. [Revi-Daniels]

Crystal Art Glass, Cambridge, Ohio. Twentieth century paperweights. [Melvin]

Crystal Brook. Germany. Trademark active
1970s. Table and gift wares. [G & T]

Crystal Cut Glass Co., Honesdale, Pa. circa
1913-19. Glass cutting shop.
Has also been attributed to Chicago
c. 1873-1907. The Chicago attribution is
doubtful. [Revi]

The Patent Crystalline Glass Works, London.
Maker of crystalline glass. Trademark
registered 1883. [Manley]

Stephimus Hedges, London. Trademark registered 1886. [Manley]

Crystal Glass Co., Bagley & Co. Ltd.
England. Trade name active c. 1960s. [BGD]

CRYSTALTYNT

Crystolyne Cut Glass Co., Brooklyn, N.Y.
Trademark for brilliant cut glass. [Revi]

Carolyn Mollie Smith, 1970s-80s, USA.
Paperweights. [Selman]

    Sig.: cane.

Christian C. Schroeder (working 1730-1760),
the Hague & Delft. Flat panes of glass
w/wheel engraved portraits after 17th century artists. [Weiss]

C. SCHROEDER, DELFT 1754

C. T. Ham Mfg. Co., Rochester N. Y.
Trademark registered c. 1887. [Peterson]

    Sig.: acid etched stenciled on lighting
wares.

"C. T. HAM/MFG. CO. NO."
followed by lamp number

Jones, McDuffee & Stratton, Boston, Mass.
Label on lighting wares. Registered
c. 1880. [Peterson]

Fort Pitt Glass House, Pittsburgh, Pa.
Circa 1834-1856. [Innes]

    Sig.: window pane with name molded in
upper and lower case block letters

CURLING & ROBERTSON

C. Vessière.   Nancy, France.   After 1920.
Used on cameo vase.   [Neuwirth]

    Sig.: on the side in cameo.

    engraved on bottom of same vase

See: Carl V. Helmschmied and C. F. Monroe.

    Reported also as a forgery, molded in   C.V.H.
    ware.   [Cronin]

See: Carl Moritz von Scheidt, Berlin.   Fine   C. V. S.
painting of city views.   C. 1820s.

D

Verrerie d'Art de Lorraine, Désiré Christain, France, c. 1880s-90s. [Traub]

Dominique Durand, N.Y., N.Y. Patent registered 1872. Glass silvering process with sealant added to Petitjean's method. Trademark, label. [Peterson]

Dom Gregorius de Wit, Holland. Active designer from about 1927 to 1945 at Leerdam for liturgical glass. [Leerdam]

Delmo & Debbie Tarsitano, active 1978, USA. Paperweights of fruit, flowers, reptiles, vegetables.

   Sig.: initial cane before 1980

Attributed to an unidentitfied diemaker for pressed pattern glass in Birmingham, England. Active circa 1837. [Wakefield]

   Sig.: molded in border pattern of pressed glass plate.

D

John & Elizabeth Degenhart, founders of
Crystal Art Glass Co., Cambridge, Ohio.
Active 1947-78. Inexpensive line of paperweights, small decorative objects. Molds
bought by Island Mold Co. and "D" removed.
Some pieces still made with "D" to support
the Degenhart Museum. [Warman/AGR]

    Sig.: molded

Variety Glass Inc., Cambridge, Ohio.
Purchased glass presses from Cambridge
Glass Company. Maker of novelty glass.
[Melvin]

    Sig.: Degenhart. Initial distinguishes   D
    factory where paperweight is cased.

Dominion Glass Co., Ltd., Montreal, Canada.
Trademark active c. 1970s. [AGR]

    Containers

    Tableware

Dugan Glass Co., successor to Northwood,
active from 1904 to 1913. [McDonald]

    Sig.:   "D" in a lozenge
                                        with overlapping bars

Salvador Dali, (b. 1904) international
painter, leader of surrealist school.

    Sig.: signed in eye of pâte de verre
    sculpture designed for Daum of France.

Louis Damon (d. 1947), France. 1900 won
silver medal for carved vases. Retailer/
designer, commissioned blanks from Daum.
[Arwas/Venzmer]

   Sig.: engraved on bottom of cameo vase

Danbury Mint, USA. Limited edition crystal
sculptures, c. 1978.

Believed to be signed

Dansk Designs, France. Mid- to late-20th
century.

   Sig.: block letters 4mm. high, etched on
   foot of stemware.

DANSK DESIGNS /
FRANCE / 1 HQ

Darboy. Unidentified. Vase of mottled
glass with cameo carving. Probably early
20th century. [Whitlow]

   Sig.: cameo script

DARBOY

St. Louis Glassworks, France. D'Argental
is French for Münzthal. See: St. Louis.
Used from 1871 to 1918. [Arwas]

Sig.: Used on cameo vase. May be in
cameo or engraved.

Cross of Lorraine appears in various
locations, either over or under the tail
of the "L."

D'Argyl. One reference attributes this
signature to a French artist.

Sig.: cameo on cameo vase

Daum et Cie, important glass works in
France. Established in 1875. During each
period, Daum has produced a wide range of
styles. Beginning in 1969, began to make
limited edition plates. Signature may be

in enamel or cameo on side, or engraved
with gilt underfoot. [Arwas/Polak]

Until about 1895:

1895-1920:

After 1920: "France" added

1920-1960

1960 on

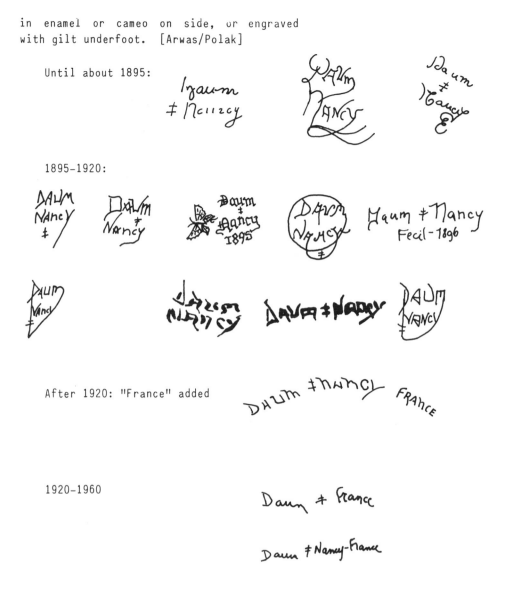

Artist signed on acid etched and enamel vase:

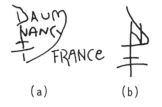

Cameo lamp (A) on base, (B) on shade

(a)   (b)

D'Aurys. Not further identified. Late 19th or early 20th century.

Signed in cameo on side near base of vase of 4 layers with three acid cuttings.

Verreries d'Art Lorraine (Verreries de Belle Etoile), France. Referenced in undated lighting fixture catalog.

Sig. inscribed on vase with molded design, c. 1925.

D'AVESN

Portland Glass Co., Portland, Maine. Active 1863-73, pressed tablewares. William O. Davis, superintendent. [Swan]

Sig.: molded

100

George Davison & Co. Ltd., Britain. Trade name for domestic and decorative ware active 20th century. [BGR]

DAVISON

See: Dominick Bieman. Also signed: "Bi," "B," "Biman," "Bimann." "D. Bimann" used after 1830. [Weiss]

D. B.,

D. BIEMAN,

D. BIMAN

D. BIMAN

D. BIMANN

De Backer, retailer about 1928-30, of object made from glass by Schneider. [Klesse-Mayr]

Sig.: under foot with matt etching; diamond point "Schneider" on foot

DÉ BACKER

Desiré Christian (1846-1907). C. 1896, left Burgun, Schverer to establish glass works in Meisenthal, Lorraine, France. Art glass designer. Also see: Burgun, Schverer et Cie. [Taub]

Signed intaglio on body of cameo vase.

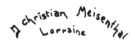

same vase signed in cameo on base:

CHRISTIAN / FECIT

Other signatures:

Acid etched sunburst with diamond point
signature

François Émile Décorchemont (1880-1971),
France. 1902 established glass works, made
pâte de verre (1905-10) with insects and
florals. C. 1912, pâte de cristal, massive
style. Worked in cire perdue. [Arwas]

Sig.: impressed on underside

Made for Décorchemont's wife.   M A

Numbers on bottom in diamond point
indicate production period:

  1903-1909   Number & letter
  date may be added in ink

  1910-1912   2 letters & number
  Dec. 1912-Nov. 1921   1-999
  Nov. 1921-Dec. 1924   01 - 0999
  Dec. 1924-Aug. 1927   A 1 - A 999
  Aug. 1927-Nov. 1930   B 1 - B 999
  Nov. 1930-May 1939   C 1 - C433
  1945-Jan. 1971   D 1 - D 507

  may also include cross of Lorraine

Deutsche Gasgluhlicht Actien Gesellschaft,
Berlin, Germany. Trade name c. 1902, for   DEGEA
lighting accessories, acid stamped.
[Peterson]

Degué.   France, early 20th century. Not further identified. [Blount/
Arwas]

> Sig.: Used on ceiling fixture of two
> layer cameo, signed near edge in cameo.
> Also used in cameo on cameo vase.

> May be engraved; more often acid etched
> w/stencils.

> Also, seen signed in diamond point on
> centerpiece of glass blown into metal
> mold.

Degué

Degué

Wilhelm Kralik Sohn, Austria-Hungry.

> Sig.: used on an iridescent vase.
> [Arwas/Blount]

De Kralik

De l'Arte, Nancy, France. Used on cameo
vase, probably late 19th or early 20th
century. [Arwas]

DE L'ARTE/NANCY

André DeLatte, Nancy, France. Circa 1921,
founded glass works for cameo and other art
glass. Also, see A. DeLatte. [Arwas]

> Signed in cameo on vase

ADELATTE NANCY

Signed in enamel on Art Deco vase, circa
1930

de l'Hommel.   Engraver in diamond point, Netherlands, 18th century. [Weiss]

Signed work known

De Lucèce.   Signed on Art Deco enameled scent bottles. [Auction]

DE LUCECE

Delux, Inc., USA. 20th century. Printed label on a Bristol-type opaque vase with handpainted flowers.

Dema Glass Ltd., Britain. Standard weight tumblers, tots, & stemware. Trade name active circa 1970s. [DBG]

DEMA

Demuth Glass Division, Brockway Glass Co., Parkersburg, W. Va. Trademark active c. 1970s [AGR]

Désiré Christian, Meisenthal, France. See: D. Christian.

   Sig.:   diamond point

George Despret (1862-1952). Glass maker at Jeumont (Nord), France. Early work was overlay with air bubbles. After 1890s, made pâte de verre. Works destroyed in World War I, re-opened 1920, closed 1937. [Arwas]

104

Sig.: sometimes w/serial number lightly
scratched on base.

Desprez, Paris, c. 1790 until at least
1830. By 1819, making cameos embedded in
crystal. [Weiss/Cloak]

    Sig.: impressed on back of sulphide
plaque, c. 1800

    Cameo sulphide, late example.

DESPREZ

DESPREZ /
RUE DES RÉCOLETS
NO. 2 À PARIS

DESPREZ FILS ET
LAMARRE

De Vilbiss, Toledo, Ohio. Perfume bottles,
Art deco dresser sets, etc. designed by
Villamot, trained at Paris Beaux Arts.
Later manufacturer of industrial pumps.
[Bird]

    Sig.: etched block letters on base.

DE VILBISS

DeVeay. 20th century. Not further identified. [Blount]

    Signed in cameo on a scenic overlay
cameo vase.

DeVez. Pseudonym of Camille Tutré de
Varreux, designer at Cristallerie de Pantin
from 1910. [Blount/Arwas]

    Signed in cameo on cameo vases.

Albert Harry Guest, Stourbridge, England.
Trademark registered in 1920. [Manley]

Daniel Henriquez de Castro (active 1830,
died 1863), Amsterdam. Amateur diamond
point engraver in Wolff's manner. Chemist
and collector of David Wolff's work.
[Weiss]

D. H. d. C.

Dial Glass, Britain. Trademark active
1960s for fancy and industrial glass, and
lighting items. [BDG]

    Trade name

DIAL

    Etched on lamp

Pope Cut Glass Co., N.Y., N.Y. Trademark
inactive by 1915. Brilliant period glass
cutting shop. [Revi]

R. E. Dietz Co., N.Y., N.Y. Trademark
circa 1890 for lighting device. [Peterson]

Cristallerie et Verrerie de Vianne, France.
Trade name for atomizers. Trade name
active 20th century.

DIFFUSEURS

Dihl, France.

Signed in script on sulphide paperweight.

DIHL

Dillon Clarke (b. 1946.), England. Worked
at "The Glasshouse," Covent Garden. Taught
sculpture.

DILLON - MAY 1970,
LONDON

Dingwall, Canada. Late 19th or early 20th
century. Retailer of cut glass for Gundy
Clapperton. [Boggess]

Sig.: etched

Di Pede. [Auction]

Signed in cameo on a double overlay
chandelier.

DI PEDE

E. D. Dithridge, Allegheny, Pa. C. 1866-
1905, trademark for general line, including
jars, lamps, etc.

See: Daum, Nancy, France.

Sig.: Used on foot of lamp decorated
with engraving and enamels. [Bloch]

D N

Reported to be a forged signature either
engraved or paper label on Tiffany type
glass. [Cronin]

D. NASH/TIFFANY & CO.
NEW YORK

Dorflinger Glass Works, White Mills, Pa. Active 1852–1921. Founded by Christian Dorflinger (1828–1915), born and trained in France. Maker of very fine cut and other glass. [Revi/McKearin/Cronin]

(a) Trademark

(b) Fake

Dominik Biemann (1800–57), Franzenbad, Bohemia. Worked in Vienna and Prague. Engraved scenes and portraits. Many spellings of name. [Weiss]

DOMINIK BIEMANN

David Donaldson. Sculptures, vessels, 1970s–80s. Formerly curator of contemporary glass at Corning; curator at Morse Gallery of Art. Studied under Harvey Littleton.

Sig.: diamond point

Donaldson 70

Société Anonyme Français des Verrerie Doyne, Le Nouvion-en-Thierache, France. Trade name for decorative items and tablewares active 1970s.

DOYNE

See: Desprez. Sulphides. [Cloak]

D P

Drehobl Bros. Art Glass Co., Chicago, Ill., USA. Established 1919. Stained glass windows, leaded lamp shades, leaded panels for pianos and jukeboxes. [Darling]

Sig.: painted

M.G.
DREHOBL Bros

Dr. Jaromir Spacek (b. 1911), Czech. Since 1936 headmaster, Glass Trade School, Novy Bor and at Kamenicky Senov. Patented 13 processes for oven decorating glass, one of which is "Bor Glass."

Sig.: Title may also appear with signature.

DR. SPACEK 1961

Delmo and Debbie Tarsitano, active 1978. Makers of paperweights. See: monogram "D-"

Sig.: before 1980, initial cane

DT

After 1980, cane at edge of design

DT

Tomlinson & Co., Manor Flint Glass Works, Barnsley, England. Glass manufacturer. Trademark registered 1891. [Manley]

Dr. Antonio Salviati, c. 1859, established his own glass house; bought out in 1886. In 1871, his firm became known as the Venice and Murano Glass and Mosaic Co. In 1877, he left to form his own company. [Newman]

Sig.: Paper label

Duc A. de Caranza, designer. See: Henri
Copillet et Cie., Noyon, France. Used on
opaque glass w/metallic iridescence for
bowls   and   vases.   Mid-1890s   to   1904.
[Arwas]

DUC. A de CARANZA

Duguersil.   Paris.   Not further identified.
  [Blount]

  Sig.: in enamel on a vase

Durand   Art   Glass   Co.,   Vineland,   N.J.
Establishec by Victor Durand (1870-1931).
Produced art glass after 1920. Iridescent
vases and iridescent shades made for non-
standard size fitter ring to fit special
lamps. [Roberts]

  Sig.:   engraved,   traced   w/aluminum
  pencil   leaving   a   silver   finish.
  Numbers on left designate shape, those
  on right height.

  Aluminum pencil in unpolished pontil of
  Cluthra vase possibly signed by Martin
  Bach, Jr. [Lagerberg]

  "K" designates Cluthra
  "Dec," decoration
  "1970," stock number
  "8," blue; "0," white, etc.

  Signed on a covered jar

1970-8/K/DEC 8

1994 V. Durand 8

Bakewel) & Pears, 19th century, Pittsburgh,
Pa.

  Sig.: on sulphide portrait of DeWitt   D W C
  Clinton, governor of Penna.   Used in a
  tumbler made about 1825.

David Wolff (1732-98), The Hague, diamond point engraving with stippling of political scene on a wine glass. Follower of Frans Greenwood. Had his own large following, thus much work referred to as "Wolff Glass." [Neuman/Weiss]

D. WOLFF 1794

E

Attributed to Jean Luce.   See: J L.
[Arwas]

Attributed to Pierre Erard, glass worker at
Stevens and Williams, England, circa 1890.
Also attributed to Edward Webb, Whitehouse
Glass Works, Wordsley, England, circa
1851-72 [Manley] or manager of Whitehouse
Glass Works, Stourbridge, circa 1885
[Revi].
Also, attributed to Ensell, retailer [and
decorator(?)], Stourbridge, early 19th cen-
tury. [Manley]

   Sig.: painted on pontil. Used on bowl
   with applied decoration

Johannes Eisenloeffel, (1876-1957) Holland.
Designer at Maastricht. [Van der Meer]

Ercole Barovier. (1889-1974) [Grover]

   Sig.: stenciled on vase with applied
   glass decoration

   May also be used with title.

E BAROVIER

E BAROVIER/MURANO

Arthur Pontefract, York, England. Ebor
Works. Glass manufacturer. Trade name
registered 1895. [Manley]

EBOR GLASS A. Pontefract WORKS YORK

E. Chapelle, France. Designer and maker of
wrought iron armatures used with blown
glass for figural lamps of glass supplied
by Muller Frères, Lunéville, France
(1895-1914). [Arwas]

    Sig.: inscribed on base of wrought iron
    rim of glass and iron figural lamp.

E CHAPELLE/NANCY

Eda Glassworks, Sweden (1833-1953).
[Auction/Newman]

    Sig.: inscribed on base of heavy clear
    vase with engraved design.

Eda

Edelstein. Bavaria area of Germany. Gift
ware trademark active late 20th century.
[T&G]

Edelstein

Edmund Hugh, USA. Limited edition paperweights, c. 1973-76. [Kovel]

Believed to be signed

Edris Eckhardt (b. 1910), USA. Cire perdue
sculptures and experiments w/laminated
gold. [Grover]

    Sig.: Occasionally date, title, and
    "United States" used with signature.

Edris Eckhardt

Edvin Ohrstrom, independent glass worker,
20th century.   Formerly with Orrefors.
[Grover/Newman]

Erwin Eisch (b. 1927), Bavaria, Germany.
Factory in Frauenau built by father and
uncle.   Contemporary craft productions.
Active 1970s. [Klesse-Mayr]

   Sig.: used on free-form vase.
May also use date.

E. Enot, Paris.   Active end of 19th century, retailer of glass ware. [Arwas]

   Sig.: underside of cameo vase. Design
attributed to Eugene Michel, 1890s.

   E. ENOT/
   6 R CHAUVEAU LAGARDE/
   PARIS

See: Gallé

O. F. Egginton Co., Corning, N.Y. Circa 1899-1920. Very fine cut glass in the brilliant period style. [Revi]

Rheinische Glashütten, Köln: Ehrenfeld, Germany Active 1864-1931. Iridescent, Art Nouveau, reproductions of 16th and 17th century designs, and tableware. [Newman]

Trademarks

(b) etched under foot of covered pokal, circa 1888

(a)   (b)

Eickhoff. Active 1982.

Signed in diamond point on base of paperweight.

Glashütte Valentin Eisch, Frauenau, Germany. Active 1970s, tableware. See: E. Eisch.

Emil Kromer (b. 1898), Steinschönau. Engraver of classical vignettes. [Pazaurek]

EK

Edinburgh Crystal Glass Co., Britain. Established 1864. Large manufacturer of cut lead crystal glasswares, trademark active 1970s. [DBG]

E & L

Grossherzogliche Edelglasmanufaktur, Darmstadt, Germany. Established 1907 by Grand

Duke Ernst Ludwig of Hesse-Darmstadt. Director: Josef Emil Schneckendorf (1865- 1949), pioneer in Art Nouveau style. Iridescent glass produced circa 1907-11. [Weiss]

Sig.: Used from 1904 to 1911

Used from 1907 to 1910

On underside of iridescent vase.

On side of same vase.

Ernst Baptiste Léveillé, Paris. Pupil and successor of Rousseau. Circa 1885, continued under name: Léveillé-Rousseau. Art Nouveau designs with internal crackled glass, etc. [Klesse-Mayr/Arwas]

Sig.: circa 1880s

After 1885; diamond point on bottom

Elisabeth Hütte Bleikristallglaswerk, Germany. Trademark active 1970s for 24% lead crystal glassware. [EGD]

ELISABETH-HÜTTE

116

Gowans, Kent & Co. Ltd., Canada. c. 1900-1911. Brilliant cut glass. Advertised that every piece was trademarked. [Boggess/Stevens]

Elizabeth Crama, active last quarter 17th century, Holland. Engraved on goblets with diamond point. [Newman]

    Signed on cover of goblet.   Signed work known

Elric. Late 19th or early 20th century. Not further identified. Two color overlay w/cameo classical decoration. [Whitlow]

    Signed in script on vase.   ELRIC

McFaddin & Co., N.Y., N.Y. Lighting accessories, circa 1909. Trademark molded in ware. [Peterson/Catalogue]   **EMERALITE**

Eugène Michel, circa 1867, worked at Rousseau's. Early 19th century established own glass works. Glass engraver in intaglio & cameo. Fine quality wares, not commercial quality signed, "Michel Nancy" or "Michel Paris." [Arwas/Hilschenz]

    Sig.: engraved on bottom

See: Gallé

Wide variety of styles, engraved, cameo, or enameled

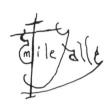

Macbeth—Evans, Pittsburgh, Pa., c. 1894. Lamp chimneys of first quality lime glass, same as "Crescent" but packed in corrugated tubes or hay. [Catalogue]

   Sig.: etched

Empire Cut Glass Co., N.Y., N.Y. & Flemington, N.J. Established before 1895, sold to Fry 1904. Cut glass of the brilliant period in standard patterns. [Revi]

   Trademark

Bolton Son & Robinson, Morsey Flint Glass Works, Warrington, England. Trademark registered 1869.

EMPRESS

J. A. Phillips & Co., Birmingham, England. Glass manufacturers. Trade name registered 1910. [Manley]

ENDAY

Ennion. Glass maker first quarter of first century A. D., believed to be Syrian and to have worked in Italy. [Newman]

Sig.: marked on pad on handle of vessel.

"ENNION" in Greek or Latin letters.

Some bear additional mark

SIDON

Ercole Barovier (1889-1974). Circa 1936, founded Barovier & Toso Glassworks, Murano, Italy. Custom made chandeliers, ornamental objects. Ercole was chief designer. Designed sculptural vessels. [Newman/-Grover]

Sig.: may also include date

Ercole Barovier

Ericot. Signed in cameo on cameo vase. Probably misread for "E. Rigot." [Auction]

ERICOT

Erie Glass Mfg. Co., Park Ridge, Ill.
Trademark active circa 1970s [AGR]

ERIE ⬛ GLASS

E. Rigot (b. 1885) chief glass designer at
Villeroy & Boch factory at Wadgassen
(Saar), Germany from 1929 to 1931. Estab-
lished in 1824.   It was one of the
companies to merge and form Villeroy and
Boch in 1836. Produced mostly tableware,
some art glass imitations of early style.
About 1902-1934, made 2-layer acid etched
cameo designs of floral and plant motifs.
[Arwas]

   Sig.: etched, used circa 1929-1931

   May also include Villeroy & Boch monogram.

E. Rigot
V.B

Erik S. Hoglund (b. 1932), glass sculptor.
Started at Boda Glassworks, Sweden, in
1953. [Auction/Grover]

   Sig.: may also include title.
   See: Boda

ERIK HOGLUND/
BODA 25-8-1970

ERIK HOGLUND/
MADE 23-8-70
10 SWEDISH GLAS

Max Erlacher, Corning, N. Y. Opened own
shop in Corning. Formerly, engraver at
Corning Glass Works. Engraves vases in
classical style. Circa 1973, made limited
edition paperweights. [Kovel/Farrar]

Believed to be signed

François Eugene Rousseau (1827-1891), France. Retired in 1855. Developed many new glass working techniques. Designed in the Art Nouveau style. [Arwas/Grover]

> Sig.: may also include number such as "1886"; diamond point under foot, may include date, scroll motif is gilt, circa 1880's

E Rousseau Paris

E Rousseau Paris.

Erskin Glass & Mfg. Co., Whellsburg, West Virginia. Trademark active circa 1970s. [AGR]

Emil Rudolph Weiss (1875-1942), Germany. Circa 1895-96, member of "Pan." [Uecker]

> Signed on overlay glass w/etched land-scape on illuminated lamp base made c. 1900.

E. R. WEISS

Escalier de Cristal. Retail and decorator shop, Paris. Established before 1874 by Charpentier. Continued by his widow. Specialized in glass furniture, decorative glass objects in metal mounts. Glass made at Vonêche Glassworks. [Bloch/Klesse-Mayr]

> Sig.: etched against a mat ground on bottom of cameo vase.

ESCALIER de CRISTAL. PARIS

Gallé's initials on same vase

E ✝ G

Signed under foot of vessel

Escalier de Cristal Paris

E. Scarpa. Art form patchwork vase, c. 1950. [Auction]

    Sig.: engraved.

E. SCARPA

Etling. Retailer in Paris. Commissioned art works from designers such as Hiez, Béal, Delabasse, and others. Pieces are molded, usually frosted finish of greyish tone. [Arwas/Auction]

ETLING
FRANCE

    Sig. molded on base of vase probably circa 1934.

E ETLING/34/FRANCE

Eugène Camot Frères, circa 1909, France. [Hilschenz]

    Sig.: relief etched on side at base of etched and engraved vase

Eug·Camot
09

Société Française de Verrerie Mecanique Champenoise, Reims, France. Trade name for goblets, vases, etc. [ANV]

EUROPGLAS

Eva Englund (b. 1937), Sweden. In 1964, began as designer for household and decorative ware at Pukebergs Glasswork. [Auction]

EVA ENGLUND 1971

E. Varnish & Co., London. Licensee of F. Hale Thomson's patent of 1849 for double-walled glassware, the interior walls lined with silver. [Revi/Newman]

    Sig.: impressed on the plug for the hole that seals the silver in.

E. VARNISH & CO.

Edward Rorke & Co., N.Y., N.Y. Trademark
c. 1877 for lighting accessories. [Peter-
son]

EVENING STAR

E. Vanda (?). Could also be "Wanda." Not
identified. Used on a cameo vase. [Blount]

F

See: Fred Carder. Designer at Steuben.
[Gardner]

    Sig: incised in models for cire perdue
sculptures and unique pieces.

Franz Fritsche, engraver for Lobmeyr.
[Davis]

    Sig.: etched on engraved plate
c. 1870-85.

Foster-Forbes Glass Co, Marion, Ind.
Trademark active 1970s. [AGR]

See: Fostoria. Trademark active c. 1909.
Label on tableware. [Peterson]

Welsbach lamp chimney. [Catalog]

    Etched signature.

Fachschule Steinschönau (Trade School),
Bohemia.

F. Treball, Langenau. Glass engraver.
[Pazaurek]

Fachschule für Glasindustrie (Trade School
for Glass), Zwiesel, Bavaria, Germany.
Used about 1910. [Pazaurek]

   Sig.: etched under the foot.

Fairmont Glass Works, Pittsburgh, Pa.
C. 1889. [Kovel]

James Alexander Forrest & Son, Liverpool,
England. Glass manufacturer. Trademark in
use about 1861.

Federal Glass Co., Columbus, Ohio. Depression glass and gift wares. Trademark
active 1970s and earlier. [Kovel]

   Molded in glass.

Not identified. Used on an iridescent vase
with painted decorations. Europe,
c. 1880-1900.

   Sig.: about 3 mm. high, molded in glass.

F

Johann Ludwig Faber, active 1678-97.
Nuremberg, Germany. Hausmaler, painted in
schwarzlot; invented new transparent enamels. One signed piece known.

Signed work known

L. C. Tiffany. Early spelling of "Favrile" glass, used on paper labels. See: L. C. T. or Louis Comfort Tiffany. [McKean]

FABRILE

Bruno Mauder (1877-1944), designer in Art Nouveau style using natural motifs. Instructor at Zwiesel Fachschule (trade school), Bavaria, Germany, c. 1910. [Newman]

Sig.: in gold on base, "Entwurf Bruno Mauder Ausführung: Fachschule Zwiesel."

Cristallerie de Champagne, Verrerie /Bayel. Trade name active 1970s. [ANV]

FAINS

Price's Patent Candle Co. Ltd., London, Battersea, & Cheshire, Eng. Patented c. 1884, label used on lamps. [Peterson]

FAIRY

Samuel Clarke (1886-1892), London. Candle maker. Patented the small base and shade to use with long-burning night candles. Licensed glassmakers to produce the shade. [Newman/Manley]

FAIRY LIGHT

Falchi. Limited edition paperweight, active 1975.

Believed to be signed

Verrerie Mecanique Champenoise, France. Trade name, active 20th century.

FAMILIA-WISS

Stratton & Co. Ltd., Britain. Decorated glass ware. Trade name active c. 1970. [BGR]

Franz Anton Pelikan (1786-1858), Meisterdorf, Bohemia. Engraved horses and hunting scenes on Biedermeier glass. [Weiss]

F. A. PELIKAN

Tiffany Furnaces, Corona, N. Y. [McKean/ Koch]

Trademark registered 1902. Used only as a label. Never etched on glass wares.

Patented 1912. Trade name not used as a permanent mark on "Fabrique" glass panels in lamp shades.

Favrilefabrique

Intaglio stamped on frame of blown glass lighting fixture in Art Nouveau style from Tiffany's home, Laurelton Hall.

FAVRILITE

Frederick Carder (1863-1963), designer with Stevens and Williams, England, from 1880 to 1903. Left Stevens & Williams to come to USA and make glass blanks for Hawkes Glass Works. Established Steuben Glass Works, Corning, N.Y.

Sig.: used on cameo vase made while at Stevens & Williams

F. CARDER, S & W

F. CARDER 1897

F. Carder

Other signatures of various sizes and styles engraved with wheel on flexible shaft. May include date.

"F. CARDER"
with fleur de lis
F. CARDER/AURENE/
STEUBEN

127

Used on "Diatreta" pieces; wheel engraved with flexible shaft, letters of
various size with or without date

F. Carder
1955

Similar style signature found on pieces
dating from 1903 to 1932. "Late
signatures" made with flexible shaft
engraving tool added by Carder for
collectors. Often forged.

J Carder

F. Carder

François Christian, Meisenthal, France,
circa 1900. Also used for Frères Christian. Art Nouveau cameo wares. [Klesse-
Mayr]

    Sig.: engraved under base

F. Christian
Meisenthal
Loths

Follett & Clarkson Osler, Birmingham, England. Established 1807.

    Sig. molded in frosted solid glass bust
    portraits.

F & C OSLER /
1 MAY 1845

Friedrich Egermann (1777-1864), Haida, Bohemia. Developed and produced Lithyalin
glass from 1828 to 1840. Discovered new
methods of staining glass red and yellow.
[Newman]

    Sig. enameled beaker

F. E.

Frederick Engelbert Kny, Bohemia. Also
worked in England c. 1860s at St. Dennis
Glassworks. Engraved in rock crystal and
intaglio styles.

F. E. K.

Félix Gilon. Designer for Albert Dammouse.
Active 1900.

    Signature used on piece with pâte
d'émail insets in pâte de verre.
[Arwas]

FÉLIX GILON /
ALBERT DAMMOUSE

Fenton Art Glass Co., Williamstown, W. Va.
Founded 1907 by Frank L. Fenton. Circa
1920s, made carnival, stretch, opalescent,
and other inexpensive art glass. Introduced limited edition lines: 1970, plates &
steins; 1975, bells; 1978, vases. [G & T]

    Sig. 8 mm long, molded in glass.

Ferdinand von Poschinger, designer at Buchenau Glashüttenwerk, Germany circa 1900.

    Sig.: incised in gilt on iridescent
glass vase with colored threads: "Ferd.
von Poschinger/Buchenau/N 224."

Frans Greenwood (1680-1764), Dorchester &
Rotterdam/Dordrecht. First to decorate
exclusively by stipple. From 1722, copied
mezzotints of contemporary flower & fruit
paintings, and Callot figures. [Weiss]

F. GREENWOOD FECIT 1764

F. Gubisch. Early 20th century, lampshade
painter at Handel. [Grant]

F. GUBISCH

Heinrich Friedrich Halter, Magdeburg, Germany. Active 1700 to 1720. Engraved
decorative goblets with landscapes & portraits. [Weiss]

F H

Fritz Heckert, worked 1866–1900, Petersdorf, Bohemia. In 1866, operating a glass
decorating shop; in 1899 a glass factory.
Up to 1890, made humpen decorated with
copies of wood engravings. Also, made
glass wares blown into wire frame.
[Neuwirth]

Sig.: In cameo on vase of three layer
with one acid cutting.

On same vase: "M R" for Max Rade, in
black enamel.

Signed in black enamel under foot in
polished pontil of iridescent vases with
gilt and enamel decoration. Designer
not identified.

F. H.
426/W.

F. H I
491/4

MR III.

MR.

F H.
501/5.

F. H 495/2.

Lp. 90.

Paper label

F. Hale Thomson, patentee of Varnish's
process for silvered glass, c. 1849. Used
double walled vessels made by James Powell
& Sons, Whitefriars Glass Works, Eng.
Walls of vessel were filled with silver and
plugged.

Sig.: impressed on disk-like plug.

F. HALE THOMSON

Steinschönau Trade School, Bohemia circa
1918, trademark.

Chance Bros. Ltd., England. Trade name for table glass, active c. 1970s. [EGD]

FIESTA

Fischer. Limited edition paperweights, circa 1970s, perhaps later. [Kovel]

Believed to be signed

F. Kretschmann worker at Thomas Webb, circa 1886. [Auction]

    Sig.: used on cameo portrait. May also appear with date.

F. KRETSCHMANN

Unidentified designer at the Wiener Werkstätte, circa 1916. [Auction]

    Signed on a commemorative enamelled beaker.

F L

Johann Flink (1801-1874), Karlsruhe, Germany. [Weiss]

FLINK

Duncan and Dithridge, N.Y.,N.Y. Jobber for cut glass makers, early 1900. Trade name for intaglio cut floral designs. [Revi]

FLORAL CRYSTAL

Lazarus & Rosenfeld, c. 1900, distributors of Bohemian ware imitating cameo glass: painted with a creamy tone, dull enamel. [Revi]

    Sig.: stenciled on bottom in block letters.

FLORENTINE ART CAMEO

Curling's Fort Pitt Glass Works, Pittsburg, Pa., c. 1830-35.

FORT PITT

Sig.: molded in cup plate

Fostoria Glass Co., Moundsville, W. Va. One of largest makers of hand-made glass in USA. Founded 1887 at Fostoria, Ohio, moved to W. Va. when local gas supply was exhausted. Trade name registered c. 1891 and 1927.

Used as a label.

Fostoria

C. 1971, introduced limited edition plates.

Frank Piggott, Australia, c. 1880s, engraver. [Graham]

Sig.: On underside of engraved tumbler.

F P / WEBB

F. P. Zach, designer for Steigerwald's Neffe, Munich, Germany. Active 1850s to 1880s. [Revi]

Sig.: diamond point on engraved polka

F. P. ZACH.

Francis Collins, Dublin, Ireland. Retailer in 1780s.

Sig.: Molded in bottom of decanters. [Wills]

FRANCIS COLLINS / DUBLIN

Frances Stewart Higgins (b. 1912). Independent glass sculptor, worked 1970s.

FRANCES HIGGINS, 1971 / with title

Franconia, Germany. Trade name active 1970s for table and gift ware. [G & T]

FRANCONIA

Franklin Flint Glass Works, succeeded by Gillinder & Sons. Philadelphia, Pa. Established and registered trademark in 1861. Closed in 1930. General line table and illuminating items. [McKearin/Peterson]

FRANKLIN

Franklin Mint, Franklin Center, Pa., USA. Established 1960s by Joseph Segel & Gilroy Roberts. Ltimited edition lines introduced in 1976 for sculptures, paperweights, plates and bells. [Kovel]

Believed to be signed

Frans Greenwood (1680-1761), Rotterdam. Stipple engraver, copied mezzotints of fruit and flowers and Callot figures. [Weiss]

Fans Greenwood fec

Franz Josef Palme. Bohemian glass engraver of animals at Thomas Webb and Sons, from 1882. [Newman]

Signed work known

Imperial Glass Co., Bellaire, Ohio. Established 1901, bankrupt 1931. Reorganized as Imperial Glass Corp.

Trademark registered 1924, used for lustered ware: undecorated with a mirror finish, decorated with a matt iridescent finish. Believed only used as a label

Frederick Carder. Founder of Steuben Glass Works. [Gardner]

Sig.: of various sizes engraved on intarsia items c. 1930.

Sig.: used on acid cut back vase.

FREDRK. CARDER/STEUBEN

Frederick Engelbert Kny, from Bohemia, worked at Whitefriars, later Stourbridge, then about 1875 to 1879 at Thomas Webb. Engraved the Elgin vase in cameo. [Beard]

FREDERICK KNY

Franz Gottstein, Gutenbrunn, Austria. Worked 1810-30: at Strang Glassworks in Moravia; c. 1823-80 at Gutenbrunn. [Weiss]

FR. GOTTSTEIN FEC. GUTENBRUNN 1830

Friedrich Egermann (1777-1864), Haida, Bohemia. Developed and produced Lithyalin glass from 1828 to 1840. Discovered new method of staining glass red and yellow. [Weiss]

FRIED. EGERMANN

William Fritsche, Bohemian who worked at Thos. Webb & Son, introduced rock crystal style engraving. Exhibited at Paris Exposition c. 1878. [Newman]

Signed work known

H. C. Fry Glass Co., Rochester, Pa. C. 1901-34, glass works & cutting shop for fine quality brilliant cut glass, and "Foval."

Trademark. Not used as signature

Sig.: acid etched on cut glass

Reported to have been forged. Watch for incorrect size or blotchy lines, and quality of glass.

Fachschule Steinschönau, Bohemia. Oldest Glass Trade School, established 1849. Trademark used c. 1911 under Prof. Beckerta. [Novy]

Fachschule Steinschönau, c. 1930 under Prof. Görlicha. [Novy]

Fachschule Zwiesel, Bavaria, Germany. [Bröhan]

   Sig.: painted or engraved, usually on outside of foot

F. P. Zach, worked at F. Steigerwald Co., Munich, Germany c. 1857. Engraved overlay glass designs. [Revi]

F. Zitzmanr (1840-1906), Steinach, Thüringen, Germany. Glass blower and lamp worker; designer for Ehrenfeld. [Arwas]

   Sig.:

   In a lustered script on foot of a flower-form vase with lustered finish, c. 1896-1900.

G

Maker not identified. Used on a cameo
vase. [Blount]

Sig.: in cameo.

Jacobus Wilhelmus (Jaap) Gidding
(1887–1955). Free Lance designer for
Leerdam from 1926 to 1930. Designed vases,
glass-mosaics, and lamp bases. [Van der
Meer]

Gustav Kreibich, engraver at Steinschönau,
Bohemia. [Pazaurek]

Gustav Schneider, c. 1899 Wiener Kunstgewerbeschule (Vienna industrial arts
school), academic painting teacher circa
1908 at Trade School in Gablonz. Also
designer for Lobmeyr and Goldberg.
[Neuwirth]

Signed with monogram on foot

G S

also on side of same vase in monogram

F M

Gillinder and Sons, Philadelphia, Pa.
1861–1930. Trademark registered 1874 for
glassware, lighting wares, etc.
[McKearin/Peterson]

Daudt Glass & Crockery Co., Toledo, Ohio.
Trademark registered 1909 for
ornamental tablewares. [Peterson]

   Sig.: etched

Gentile Glass Works, Star City, W. Va.
Paperweights since 1959. [Melvin]

   Sig.: John Gentile.   Signed on base   G 1963
   since 1963.

Les Frères Gerard, about 1804-1825, Paris,   G
France.   Decorating   studio of secondary
importance. [Amic]

Glaswerke   Warmensteinach   GmbH,   Warmensteinach,   Germany.   Trademark   active
c. 1970s for stemware. [Körting]

S. A. Uiterwaal (1889-1960).   Circa 1930s,
designed figural pieces at Leerdam about
1930. [Leerdam/Van der Meer]

Glenshaw Glass Co., Glenshaw, Pa. Trademark
active c. 1970s. [AGR]

Cristallerie   d'Émile   Gallé   (1846-1904),
Nancy, France. Émile Gallé was a leader of
the Art Nouveau movement.   He established

his own glass house for art glass in 1867. It closed in 1931. Used marquetrie, cameo, engraving, and other techniques for vases, lamps, and tableware. Much ware was of fine quality, individually decorated. They also produced a commercial line of acid etched cameo for the popular market. [Bloch/Gardner]

Sig.: engraved, with many other variations.

Sig.: cameo, in many other variations.

138

A star beside name denotes work produced
after Gallé's death. The star was used
from September 1904 until 1914.

*Gallé

*Gallé

Richard Douglas & Co., N.Y., N.Y. Lighting
wares. Trademark registered c. 1874.
[Peterson]

Gabriel Argy—Rousseau (1885- ?), France.
Art Nouveau objects in pâte de verre and
pâte de cristal. [Arwas/Klesse-Mayr]

    Sig.: moulded in shallow relief on pâte
    de verre box

G. ARGY ROUSSEAU

6798

    Impressed under base of same pâte de
    verre box

    Others: generally molded on side

GARGY-   G . A - R
ROUSSEAU

    May include a number such as: "14358"

    G. ARGY ROUSSEAU

    G ARGY ROUSSEAU FRANCE
    G ARGY ROUSSEAU
    A. 5. BOURAINE

A. Gauthier, rue de Paradis, Paris. Active between 1906 and 1915, exact dates unknown. [ANV]

Sig.: in cameo on a cameo vase c. 1915.

GAUTHIER

Giancarlo Begotti. Active 1950s.

Sig.: on enamel and etched plaque.

G. BEGOTTI 58

Gundy-Clapperton Co., Toronto, Canada. 1905-1931. Brilliant style cut glass on blanks from Baccarat and Val St. Lambert. [Boggess]

Sig.: etched.

Mark may also have retailer's name.

Georges de Feure (b. 1868, active up to 1929), France. Moulded forms and cameo decoration. [Arwas]

Sig.: acid-stenciled script or moulded in low relief on side.

Later models are signed on the base.

See: Despret. May also be used with a number.

G. DESPRET

Georges Dumoulin (b. 1882), France. Designer, used heavy bubbled glass, externally decorated. Influenced by M. Marinot. [Arwas]

Sig.: diamond point on base, c. 1920s.

G. DUMOULIN

Gebrüder Désiré und François Christian, Meisenthal, Elsass-Lothringen (Alsace/Lorraine). Art Nouveau designs c. 1900. [Klesse-Mayr/Taub]

Sig.: engraved underfoot of cameo vase.

Géef. Lyon, France. [Blount]

Sig.: Cameo signature on cameo decorated lamp.

Georg Ernst Kunckel (1692-1750), Gotha. Court engraver c. 1721, worked in diamond point and intaglio using motifs of festoons and trellised lambrequins. [Weiss]

G E K FEC./ A

See: Thomas Webb & Sons. Used on superior cameo carved items.

GEM CAMEO

Genet & Michon, France. C. 1920s. Decorative objects and lighting fixtures.
[Grover]

Sig.: vase carved with monkeys GENET & MICHON, FRANCE

Geno. Not further identified. Probably
France c. 1910.

Signed on a pâte de verre sculpture of a   GENO
lizard on a leaf.

Gentile Glass, Star City, W. Va. Trademark for gift ware. Limited editions
paperweights introduced c. 1973. [Kovel/
AGR]

George Bacchus & Son, Birmingham, Eng.
Established c. 1840. Influenced by Bohemian
glass. Decorated opal ware transfer printed
with black, sepia, and polychrome enamels.
[Revi/Manley]

Sig.: vase c. 1850

George Palme, decorator of glass lamp
shades at Handel early 20th century.
[Grant]

Sig.: etched in shallow cameo on Art   GEORGE PALME
Nouveau lamp shade.

Georg Friedrich Killinger (1694-1726), Nuremberg, Ger. Wheel engraving on Bohemian or Nuremberg glass. Some early work combined diamond point and wheel engraving. Deeply cut work on thick Bohemian glass superseded this style work. [Weiss]

George Henry Woodall. See: Woodall. Cameo engraver. [Webb's Crystal/Grover]

Sig.: used 1891-1918

Geo. Woodall

George woodull

George Henry Woodall

Pabst & Arming, N.Y., N.Y. Trademark registered c. 1879, lighting wares. [Peterson]

Gottfried Stadler, Switzerland. Active 1663, glass painter. [Gessert]

GF.S

Giancarlo Begotti. C. 1950s-60s.

Sig.: on enamel and etched plaque.

GIANCARLO BEGOTTI 58

G. H. Hoolaart, 17th century, Netherlands. Follower of F. Greenwood; used diamond point. [Weiss]

Signed work known

143

Gillinder & Sons, Philadelphia, Pa. Established c. 1867. Trademark registered 1883 for decorative items and lamps. [McKearin]

Sig.: molded in block letters 4 mm high, on centennial figure of a lion.

Small animals may also be reissues. Size of mark may not be the same as the old.

Reported as a forgery. Note spelling.

GILLENDAR

Trademark active c. 1970s.

Johann Ostritz (1815-1896), Haida, Bohemia. Engraver. [Weiss]

G. J. OSTRITZ

Jeannette Glass Co., Jeannette, Pa. [G & T/Stout]

Trademark registered c. 1917 for ovenware. Label or molded in glass.

Trademark active c. 1970s

Glass Crafts of America, Pittsburgh, Pa. Trademark active c. 1970s. [AGR]

Soho & Vesta Glass Works, England. Trade name registered 1887. [Manley]

GLOW WORM

Gottlob Samuel Mohn (1789-1825), Dresden/
Laxenburg. Son of Samuel Mohn (1762 to
1815). Decorated tumblers with transparent
enamel, mostly scenics framed with ornamental gilt design, silhouettes, and allegorical subjects. [Weiss/Newman]

G. MOHN F WIEN

W. Goebel, one of the Rodental group.
Issued limited edition bells and plates in
glass c. 1978. [Kovel]

  Sig.: acid stamped with date.

Carl Goldberg, glassworks, Haida, Bohemia.
Founded in 1881, still active in 1906.
Maker of fine useful and decorative items.
Made an industrial cameo and iridescent
ware. [Arwas]

  Sig.: in cameo on cameo vase.

Gill Brothers Co., Steubenville, Ohio.
Trademark patented c. 1907, for lighting
wares. [Peterson]

Gorham, one of the largest makers of sterling silver, distributor of glass and gift
ware. In 1978, introduced limited edition
paperweights. [Kovel]

Believed to be signed

A. E. O'Connor, Goshen, N.Y. C. 1902-04.
Cutting shop for brilliant period good
quality cut glass. Arthur E. O'Connor
operated The American Cut Glass Co. for his
father.

Gebrüder Pallme-König, Steinschönau, Czech.
Established in 1786. Art glass. [Arwas]

Sig.: paper label printed in black on
gold applied to art deco perfume bottle,
early 20th century

Gilbert Poillerat, sulphide designer.
[Auction]

Sig.: stamped on shoulder of sulphide in
Baccarat paperweights. Baccarat trademark acid stamped on base

G. P.

G. P. 1953

G. POILLERAT

G. POILLERAT, BACCARAT

See: Harrach. [Blount]

Sig.: engraved on 2 layer cameo vase
with acid and wheel cutting.

Graf
Harrach

Gruder, Blank & Co., Berlin, Ger. Circa
1903, trade name used on lighting wares.
[Peterson]

GRAL

Gral Glashütte GmbH, Durnau, West Germany.
Founded c. 1930 as a glass refinery. In
1938, opened subsidiary in Bohemia; 1939
added glassworks. Employed fine contemporary designers. Mouth blown and hand cut
crystal glassware. [EGD]

Trade name.

GRALGLAS

Granget. Limited edition crystal sculptures introduced in 1973. [Kovel]

Believed to be signed

G. Raspiller, Strassburg, Germany. Active circa 1910. [Blount/Hilschenz]

G. Raspiller

G. Raspiller

Sig.: in cameo on side of cameo vase.

May also have "Strassburg" included with name.

Thomas G. Hawkes & Co., Corning, N.Y. Trademark first used in 1902 for fine intaglio cut glass of the late brilliant period. [Revi]

Trademark acid etched, usually on center bottom or on side of vessel. Beware of forgeries on wrong type of glass.

Registered trade name. Has been reported to be used as an acid stamp in block letters on ware other than Hawkes.

GRAVIC

Mrs. Graydon-Stannus, London, active about 1923-32. Maker of decorative wares using opal glass, clear glass with applied decoration, cluthra, and flashed glass. Forgeries are reported. [Grover/Newman/Manley]

Gray-Stan

Crown Crystal, Australia, active c. 1936-7. Name of a cut glass pattern and a pressed pattern that simulates cut glass. [Graham]

GRIMWADE

Georg Schindler (active 1618-35), Prague. Engraver. [Weiss]

G. S.

Georg d. Ä. Schwanhardt, the elder, (1611(?)-1667), Nuremberg. Diamond point engraver. [Newman]

G. S.

Gerhard Schechinger, Schwäbisch Gmünd, Germany. Active 1960s. Sculptor. [Klesse-Mayr]

    Sig.: diamond point on base of stylized fish.

Gottfried Stadler (1616-1664), Switzerland. Glass painter active 1663. [Gessert]

G·S

Gottfried Spiller (active 1683, d. 1728), Potsdam/Silesia. In 1702, became royal engraver at Potsdam. Used a water-powered mill at Berlin works. Engraved in hochschnitt and tiefschnitt. Often used glass seven to ten millimeter thick. [Weiss]

G. SPILLER

George Sutherland, England. Engraver in diamond point. Active 1857. [Wilkinson]

    Sig.: on armorial goblet

G. SUTHERLAND / SEP. 1859

F. Gubisch. Lampshade painter at Handel, early 20th century. [Grant]

Gubisch

Guerchet. French goldsmith active c. 1895. [Hilschenz]

    Sig.: on silver overlay of iridescent glass vessel

GUERCHET ORFÈVRE 62364

    Also on glass of same vessel:

M G

Gueron Glass Works, France, c. 1920s or 1930s. Illuminated figures and night lights after designs by Cazaux. See: Cazaux. [Arwas]

    Sig.: molded. Sometimes has "France" and "Cazaux."

GUE   GUERON

GUERON GUERON
MADE IN
FRANCE   CAZAUX

Bermondsey Glass Works, England, circa 1900. [Manley]

    Signed on a molded head

GUY UNDERWOOD /
APPLIED ART

G. V. Nes, active c. 1687. Dutch engraver in diamond point. [Newman]

G. V. NES

George W. Woodall, England. Nineteenth century cameo worker. See: Woodall and Geo. Woodall. [Thos. Webbs/Grover]

G W 152 July 29, 1913

Used 1889 to 1899

G. Woodall

149

George W. Drake & Co., Corning, N. Y. C. 1898–1908. Fine glass cutting studio of the Brilliant Period. Used blanks from Corning, Dorflinger, and Pairpoint. [Farrar/Revi]

H

Harriet Bott (active 1880s-90s).

    Sig.: monogram of superimposed letters   HB
used on cameo vase

Hariet Bauer or Henry Bedigie
Both were painters of lampshades at Handel,
early 20th century. [Grant]

H. P. Berlage (1856-1934), from 1923 to
1934 designer for tableware, drinkware,
vases, and other items for Leerdam.
[Leerdam/Van der Meer]

Honesdale Decorating Co., Honesdale, Pa.
C. 1900-32, established by C. Dorflinder.
[Revi/JCK]

    Sig.: carly mark

    after 1920, used paper label.

Fostoria Glass Specialty Co., Fostoria,
Ohio. C. 1904, trademark for lighting
wares. [Peterson]

Hans Heinrich (1557–1612), Switzerland. Painted windows. [Gessert]

HE

Hans-Heinrich Wagmann (1557–1626), Switzerland. Painter of windows. [Gessert]

HW

Hans Balthasar Fisch (1608–1656), Switzerland. Painter of armorial windows. [Gessert]

H B F

Hilda Schmid-Jesser (b. 1894), working 1916–22. Member of the Wiener Werkstätte. [Auction]

Sig.: on enamel decorated stemware.

H. J.

Wiener Werkstätte monogram

WW

Pieter Holsteyn (1582–1662). Glass painter and engraver. [Gessert]

PH   PH
1627

Heinrich Zoff or Hermann Zeh
H. Zoff (b. 1859), teacher at Gablonz & Steinschönau.
Hermann Zeh (b. 1892). C. 1931 director of glass trade school at Steinschönau. [Neuwirth]

ZH

May also have additional initials that stand for Kunstgewerbe und Kunsthandwerk Fachschule Steinschönau

KK ST

Hans Klein (b. 1922), Stuttgart, Germany.

HK

Attributed to Honesdale, maker of brilliant cut glass. Mark referenced probably referred to a goblet with stem obscured. See: "Honesdale."

"H" on a shield

Architect Adolf Hegenbarth, c. 1920s, engraver at Steinschönau. [Pazaurek]

H

Fritz Heckert. See: FH. [Ptocku]

    Sig.: enameled

Royal Russian Glass Manufactory during the reign of Nicholas II. In 1894, Nicholas became Czar. [Arwas]

    Sig.: used on overlay vase with floral design, engraved under foot

A. H. Heisey & Co., Newark, Ohio. Established 1893 by Maj. A. H. Heisey; closed in 1958. Used on cut glass, pressed glass, and a wide variety of other ware. Trademark registered c. 1900.

    Sig.: molded. Many fakes, some as recent as 1984. Check quality of glass and shape of diamond. Heisey now controls all use of old molds.

Anchor Hocking Corp, Lancaster, Ohio. Wide variety of domestic items.

    Trademark.

Harvey Industries, Clarksburg, W. Va.
Trademark active c. 1970s

Hazel Atlas Glass Corp., Wheeling W. Va.
Jars and depression glass, c. 1920s on.

   Trademark molded in bottom

Hadelands Glass Works, Jevnaker, Norway.
Established c. 1762. C. 1850s began to
replace bottle production with heavy lead
crystal, and tablewares. Under influence
of the Berg family for six generations.
Most pieces signed in diamond point with
"Hadelands" and may include name or initials of designer. [Auctions/Grover/
Newman]

   Gro Sommerfelt (b. 1940), Norway.
   C. 1970s designer.
   Sig.: used on free form vase.

HADELANDS NORWAY
1971 GRO SOMMERFELT

   Jon Gundersen. Designer of abstract
   sculptures.

HADELANDS NORWAY/9.7/
JON GUNDERSEN

   Severin Brörby, designer during the
   1960s. Designs numbered in the 7,000s.

HADELANDS NORWAY/
S B   SEVERIN BRÖRBY

   Willy Johansson (b. 1921), designer at
   Hadelands since 1947. Designs numbered
   in the 2,000s.

HADELANDS NORWAY/
W J   WILLY JOHAN

   Wilhelm Johansson, father of Willy
   Johansson. Master glass blower. Works
   numbered in the 3,000s

J W J

Sverre Pettersen (1884-1959), at Hadelands from 1928.

S P

Jonas Hidle. Chief designer of lighting
wares. Designed some vessels. Pieces
numbered in the 5,000s

J H

Herman Bongard (b. 1926). At Hadeland
from 1947 to 1955. Designs numbered in
the 1,000s

H B

Arne Jon Jutrem (b. 1929). At Hadelands
since 1950. Designs numbered in the
4,000s

A J

Oertel & Co., designers for trade school at
Haida, c. 1913. [Neuwirth]

Sig.: paper label used on crystal vase
with ruby overlay.

Hailwood & Ackroyd Ltd., Morley, Leeds,
England. Nineteenth century glass works.
Used from 1920 to 1930. [Manley]

Sig.: used on opaque red vase

HAILWARE

See: F. Hale Thomson. Used on a silvered
vase. [Newman]

HALE THOMSON
PATENT LONDON

K. R. Haley Glasware Co., Greensburg, Pa.
Table and gift ware. Trademark active
c. 1970s.

United Jewelers Inc., N.Y., N.Y. Trademark
active c. 1914. [Peterson]

Gill Brothers Co., Steubenville, Ohio.
Trademark registered c. 1896 for lighting
items. [Peterson]

Handel Glass Decorating Company. Closed in
1936. Noted for decoration of reverse
painted and leaded lamp shades. Made other
glass items. [Grant]

    Sig.: On shades may be scratched or
painted on. Often with name of artist.

    On metal bases may be impressed or cast.

    After 1910, stamped into the top metal
rim of Teroca shades.

    Artists' signatures:

Mr. Anderson

Arthur Cunette

Harriet Bauer or Henry Bedigie

Not identified

John Bailey

Numbering of painted shade series:

Decorated opal ware for kerosene lamps	2,000 to 3,000
Earliest painted line series beginning about 1905	5,000
Painted shades, beginning about 1913	6,000
Painted shades beginning about 1920	7,000

Hans Mauder (1903-1970). Independent glass worker until 1931. From about 1931 to 1963, taught at Zwiesel Trade School, Bavaria. [Grover]

HANS MAUDER FACHSCHULE ZWIESEL

Harold J. Hacker, Buena Park, Calif. Paperweights. [Cloak]

Sig.: inscribed on base.

HAROLD J. HACKER 1965

Neuwelt Glass Works, Bohemia. In 1798, taken over by Graf Harrach. Became second largest manufacturer of tableware. Also made copies of Tiffany iridescent glass and many other types including the Nancy Art Nouveau school. [Arwas]

Sig.: In cameo on side of commercial quality cameo vessel of 4 layers of glass with three acid cuttings and wheel engraving.

Harvey K. Littleton, Leader of modern movement in studio glass, designed the "day" furnace. [Klesse-Mayr]

Sig.: diamond point

Design created for Val Saint Lambert

Thomas G. Hawkes & Co., Corning, N.Y.
Established by Thomas Hawkes with assistance of Frederick Carder c. 1880-1959.
Cutters of fine brilliant cut glass and tableware.

Older trademark

Sig.: 1880-90 no mark

1895-1962 later trademark form also
acid stamp

1903-1920, trade name used for intaglio
cut designs, usually fruit or flowers;
acid etched.
Early designs are copper wheel engraved;
later designs stone wheel engraved

1900-1959 acid stamp in block letters on
stemware

HAWKES

Acid etched on Verre de Soie salad
dressing bottle [Auction]

HAWKES /
PATENTED OCTOBER 6, 1914

Penrose Hawkes.   Until 1972, retailer of
glass cut by Floyd Manwarren. [Farrar]

Sig.: in script with diamond point.

HAWKES

Hobbs, Brockunier & Co., Wheeling, W. Va.
C. 1845-1863, established by John L. Hobbs
& James B. Barnes. Hobbs, Brockunier & Co.
formed by the sons of Hobbs and Brockunier
in 1863. Fine decorative glass: Peachblow,
pressed amberina, etc. [McKearin/Cronin]

Reported to appear as a forgery.

H & B CO. / WHEELING

158

Henry Bedigie.   Lampshade painter at Handel, early 20th century. [Grant]

    Sig.: used on a reverse painted lamps shade for a kerosene lamp, c. 1906.   H. BEDIGIE

H. A. Copillet et Cie.   Established by Henri A. Copillet.   In 1890s, joined by Amédée Duc de Caranza and M. Neuville. Made dark iridescent glass bowls and vases. [Arwas]

    Sig.: stencil script or capitals. May include additional signature of Duc de Caranza.

Fritz Heckert. See: F H

    Sig.: Cameo on cameo vase.

Heidelberger Bleikristall, Kisslinger, Germany.   24% lead crystal ware, active c. 1970s. [EGD]   HEIDELBERGER BLEI-KRISTALL

Heikki Orvola (b. 1943), Finland.   At Notsjö Glassworks in Nuutajärvi, Finland, since 1968. Sculptural vessels. [Grover]   HEIKKI ORVOLA NUUTAJÄRVI NOTSJO

Helen Turner Monro, 20th century British engraver, designer of ornamental and tableware for Edinburgh & Leith Flint Glass Co. [RHE]

    Sig.: diamond point engraved on horseshoe band. May include date.

F. & C. Osler, Ltd., Birmingham, England. Glass manufacturer. Trade name registered 1914. [Manley]

HELIOLITE

Macbeth-Evans Glass Co., Pittsburgh, Pa. Trademark registered circa 1892. Lighting wares. [Peterson]

    Sig.: etched

Helmut Geib, designer at Zwiezel Fachschule, Bavaria, Germany.

HELMUT GEIB F. S. ZWIESEL, 1969

Henry Braggie, lamp shade painter at Handel, early 20th century. Occasionally mis-read as "Broggie" or "Braggi."

HENRY BRAGGIE

Hermann Benckerlt, decorator in schwarzlot and en grisaille. [Weiss]

Signed work known

Hermann Schwinger (1640-1683), Nuremberg, Germany. (Weiss]

    Sig.: on a beaker decorated in diamond point. [Weiss]

HERMANN SCHWINGER INVEN

State Trade School for Glass (Staatsfachschule) in Haida, Bohemia.

    Trademark used c. 1900. [Novy]

Heinrich Frederich Halter, Magdeburg/
Brandenburg, Ger. Working c. 1700-20.
Goblets with engraved views of towns or
portraits. [Weiss]

   Sig.: in an unpolished engraved sun   H. F. H.

H. Fisher, lampshade painter at Pairpoint
Corp., New Bedford, Mass. Probably early
1900s.

   Sig.: scratched on interior of painted
shade [Auction]   *H FISHER*

Emanuel Hoffmann (1819-1878), Blottendorf/   Hfm.
Karlsbad, Bohemia. [Weiss]

Haraut-Guignard, successor to Rousseau's
business. [Bloch]

   Sig.:

Sometimes found with retailer's mark: Le Rosey

Henri-Gabriel Ibels (1867-1936), Paris.
Painter of the Nabis school. [Benezit]

   Sig.: used on leaded glass window made
of Tiffany glass and shown by Samuel
Bing. [Magazine of Art, 1898/Connois-
sseur, Dec. 1969, p. 296]   *HG Ibels*

Henry G. Richardson & Sons, Stourbridge, England. Succeeded W. H. B. & J. Richardson. Maker of art and other fancy glassware, 19th century on. [Manley]

Trademark registered 1912

Heinrich Jäger (active 1690-1720), worked in Berlin and Arnstadt, engraver in tiefschnitt and hochschnitt, and diamond point. [Weiss]

Signed on a römer.   H. I.

Stuart & Sons, Red House Glass Works, Stourbridge, Eng.   Trademark registered 1888.

Hans Jacob Dunz (d. 1649). [Gassert]

Signed on a banquet scene on glass.   H. I. DUNZ

Bryce Higbee & Co., Bridgeville, Penna. Established by John Bryce c. 1879. Table and lighting wares. [Innes]

Sig.: molded on a fruit knife

The mark is currently being reproduced.

See: Francis Higgins

L. Hinsberger Cut Glass Co., N.Y., N.Y. Glass cutting shop, Brilliant Period, active 1895-1913. [Revi/JCK]

Kristallglaswerk Hirschberg der Steinkohlenberg, Germany. Drinkware. Trademark active c. 1970s. [Kötring]

H. J. Boam, c. 1900. Possibly a worker at Thomas Webb's, England. [Wilkinson]

    Sig.: used on vessel with engraved hunting scene.

H J BOAM

    Signed on a cameo plaque.

H. J. BOAM

Harvey K. Littleton, USA. First in the United States to work glass as a craft medium. Developed a small studio day furnace. Formerly Professor at University of Wisconsin. [Grover]

    May include title and date with signature.

H K Littleton

Hanns Model, Stuttgart, Germany. Active 1972, modern form vase with cutting. [Klesse]

    Sig.: diamond point under base

HM 1972

Muller Frères, Croismare, France. Active
1900. [Hilschenz/Arwas]

Sig.: diamond point under foot of vase,
butterfly in cameo

On side of same vase in diamond point

Signature etched under foot of vase

"Lunéville" added after 1919

Henri Edouard Navarre (1885-1971), France.
Began working with glass in 1924. Designed
vessels and sculptures. [Arwas/Brohan]

Sig.: inscribed on vase with applied
decorations. Usually appears with a
number.

J. Hoare & Co, Corning, N.Y. C. 1854-1910.
Fine quality glass cutting studio of the
Brilliant Period. [Farrar/JCK/Revi]

1868-95 no trademark

1900-20, block letters, acid stamped   HOARE

See: J. H. Hoare.

Hobbs Glass Co., Wheeling, W. Va.
1845-1891. Brilliant period cut glass.
[Boggess]

Sig.: etched

Holmegaard Glassworks, Zealand, Denmark.
Established in 1825. During the 1920s,
made contemporary decorative and tablewares. Merged with Kastrup Glassworks in
1954. [Auction/Newman]

Sig.: bowl designed by Per Lütken, who
was appointed to succeed designer Jacob
Bang in 1942.

Signature on same bowl added later.

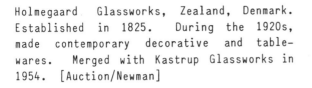

PER LUTKEN

Honesdale Decorating Co., Honesdale, Pa.
Decorating shop set up c. 1901 by Christian
Dorflinger & Sons. Closed 1932. From
1900, managed by Carl Frances Prosch.
[Revi/JCK]

Sig.: script in etched gold on base of
cased glass vase with etched and gilt
decor.

Honesdale (a)

Honesdale (b)

G. H. Hoolaart, Netherlands. Engraver in
stipple and diamond point during the 17th
century. [Weiss]

Signed work known

Hope Glass Works, Providence, R. I.,
1880-1915. Cutting shop of the Brilliant
Period. Purchased blanks from Pairpoint.
[Revi/JCK]

Houze Glass Corp., Point Marion, Pa. Trademark active 1970s. [AGR]

Hoya Crystal, Japan. Trademark active 1970s.

See: Pairpoint Glass Co. [Auction]

Signature of artist on reverse painted lamp shade. Shade attributed to Pairpoint; base signed "Pairpoint." Attributed to Henry Parlow.

H P

Hans Rudolf Egeri (1550-1593), Switzerland. Window glass painter. [Gessert]

H. R. E.

Hugh Edmund Smith, USA. Twentieth century maker of paperweights. [Selman]

Sig.: signature cane

On base of same weight in diamond point:

H. Schimpky, Germany. Active c. 1888.

Signed on a decorated humpen.

H. SCHIMPKY

Horst Stauber, Passau and Wien. Worked with the Gino Salmistari Group. Active circa 1970s. [Klesse-Mayr]

Signed with acid etching under foot of a contemporary vessel with inlay.

H. S. Williams-Thomas. Designer at Stevens
and Williams. [Stevens & Williams]

Sig.:   *H. S. Williams-Thomas.*

Helen Tynell. Designer for Riihimaen Lasi,
Oy, Finland, circa 1950s. [Auction]

Sig.: on sculpture   H. TYNELL/RIIHIMAEN LASI/OY, FINLAND

May also use title.   HELENA TYNELL RIIHIMAEN LASI

George A. Young, Portland, Maine. Trade-   HUB
mark registered 1899, etched or molded on
lighting wares. [Peterson]

Hunt Glass Co., Corning, N.Y. Active
1895-on. Used Corning Glass Works blanks
for cutting during the Brilliant period.
Presently producing table and gift wares.
[Farrar/JCK/AGR]

Sig.: script acid stamped c. 1906-15.

Later, stickers of various colors,
including pale blue and moss green.

Contemporary label

Wolfgang Huss, Hirtlback, Germany. Active
1970s. Free form sculptures.

    Sig.: diamond point under base

Hans Wessler (d. 1632). Engraver working
in Prague and Nuremberg. [Weiss]

    Sig.: engraved on glass disk   H W

Hieronimus William Fritchie (1888-1916),
Corning, Toledo, Ohio & Philadelphia, Pa.
[Farrar]

    Sig.: in diamond point script on en-   H W FRITCHIE
    graved glass

Hans Wolfgang Schmidt (active 1676-1710),
Nuremberg, Germany. Glass engraver of   H. W. S. 1679
battle scenes and ruins on drinking glas-
ses. [Weiss]

H. Zweerts, probably 18th century, Nether-
lands. Engraver in diamond point. [Weiss]   Signed work known.

I

Imperial Glass Co. Maker of commercial lines of domestic wares.

    Sig.: molded

Registered in 1951

J. & L. Lobmeyr, Vienna, Austria. Established 1823 by Josef Lobmeyr (1792-1855). Glass factory operated in Bohemia until nationalized in 1945. Wide range of engraved, iridescent, and other wares.

    Sig.: engraved on engraved bowl
    and
    Enameled on enamel decorated tumbler.

Jacob Floris (1524-81), Flanders. Glass painter. [Gessert]

Iganz Preissler (b. 1670). Hausmaler to Count Franz Karl Liebsteinsky von Kolowrat at Kronstadt 1729-39. Landscape, peasant, chinoiserie, laub-und-bandelwerk, and mythological subjects. [Weiss]

    Attribution questioned by some authors

IGNAZ PREISSLER FEC.

Islington Glass Co. Ltd., Birmingham, Eng.
C. 1860s. Paperweights. [Newman]

    Sig.: in cane   I G W

See: "H I," Heinrich Jäger   I H

I. H. Ganttinn, Switzerland.   Active c.
1628. Glass painter. [Gessert]

Lazarus (d. 1796) and Isaac Jacobs (father
and son), in 1805 established Non-Such
Flint Glass Manufactory, Bristol, Eng.
Isaac (active 1790-1835) was glassmaker to
George III. [Newman]

    Sig.: in gilt on deep cobalt blue wares.

(a)

(b)

See: "Württembergische Metallwarenfabrik."
C. 1930s. Label for glass of heavy metal
combined with colored inlays, bubbles,
patterns, and stripes. [Brohan]

Imperial Glass Co., Bellaire, Ohio. Tablewares, limited edition plates in crystal
and carnival glass, introduced in 1970.

    Sig.: molded.   trademark registered
    c. 1913

Trademark registered 1914

Trademark registered 1939. Label

Additional trademark active c. 1970s

Indiana Glass Co., Dunkirk, Indiana. Distributor of imported wares. Gift and table ware, trademark active c. 1970s [G & T]

Castleton China Co., N.Y., N.Y. Gift wares. Trademark active c. 1970s. [G & T]

Legras et Cie., St. Denis, Paris, France. "Indiana" line of cameo wares c. 1900. [Arwas]

Sig.: in gold on cameo vase with gilt decorations.

Indiana Glass Co., Dunkirk, Ind. Trademark active c. 1970s. [G & T]

See: McKee Glass Co.

Paper label c. 1916-1923. Cut glass with flower decorations.

Iorio Glass Shop, Flemington, N.Y., N.Y. Brilliant Period Cut glass. [Revi]

Joseph Piesche, Budapest, Hungary. Working
c. 1824. [Weiss]

    Signed on beaker, intaglio engraved with
    diamond cutting.

IOS. PIESCHE FC

Kent F. Ipsen (b.1933), USA. Teacher.
Sculptural vases. [Grover]

IPSEN

Fostoria Glass Specialty Co., Fostoria,
Ohio. Trademark registered c. 1910. Line
of iridescent glass shades after the style
of Tiffany. [Roberts/Peterson]

    Paper label, never permanently signed on
    shades.

Macbeth-Evans Glass Co., Pittsburgh, Pa.,
c. 1897. Etched on fine flint glass lamp
chimneys packed in square cartons.
[Catalog]

IRON CLAD
BEST
FLINT GLASS

Irving Cut Glass Co., Honesdale, Pa.
Cutting shop for fine brilliant cut glass
active c. 1900-33. Early period used
Dorflinger blanks, later Fry and Libbey
"pig-iron" blanks, the mold pressed type.
Active c. 1900-1933. Etched block letters
are not authentic. [Boggess/Daniels]

Irving

International Shade Co., Springfield, Mass.
Label on lamps c. 1912. [Peterson]

I S C O

Thomas Farrar, Manchester, Eng.   Glass
novelties.   Trade name registered 1894.
[Manley]

ISOBEL

Verreriers Domec, Bordeaux. Trade name for
decorative glass, active c. 1970s. [ANV]

ISOLEX

Not further identified.

"Istosi" on printed label on a stylized
bird., c. 1959. [Auction]

ISTOSI

Jacob Weber (1637-85), Switzerland. Glass
painter. [Gessert]

I W

I WEBER

Newton Chambers & Co., Ltd.   Sheffield,
Eng.   Glass manufacturer.   Trade name
registered 1893. [Manley]

IZAL

J

James Couper & Sons, City Glass Works, Glasgow, Scotland. Glass manufacturers. Trademark registered 1888. [Manley]

Nicolas, Josephus Antonius Hubertus Franciscus (1897-1972), in 1930, became designer of vases at Leerdam, Holland. [Van der Meer]

J. Derbyshire & Co., 1856-1893, Manchester, England. Decorative wares. [Wakefield]

Jefferson Glass Co., Follansbee, W. Va. Trademark registered 1913, impressed on lighting wares. [Peterson]

See: Professor Hoffmann [Newman]
    Sig.: monogram

James Hateley, Birmingham, Eng. Glass manufacturer. Trademark registered 1887.

Jean Luce, Paris. C. 1931 opened his own design studio for glass and ceramics, inspired by Cubism. [Arwas]

    Sig.: C. 1935, monogram, acid etched on vase.

174

Joseph Locke (1846-1936), worked in England at Hodgetts Richardson & Co., copied the Portland vase. In 1882, to New England Glass Co. C. 1889 to Libbey where he created Amberina and other types of art glass. In 1891, to United States Glass Co. Later, he opened his own shop. See: "Locke Art." [Revi/Newman]

    Sig.: monogram, superimposed letters   J L

See: John Northwood II.

    Sig.: monogram in cameo on cameo vase.   J N

John Walsh Walsh, Soho & Vesta Glass Works, Birmingham, Eng. Established in 1854. Trademark registered at later date. [Manley]

Unknown maker of Bohemian paperweights in the 19th century.   J

John Deacons, Perthshire, Scotland. Making paperweights of classical millefiori and lampwork floral, insect, and reptiles. [Selman]

    Sig.: on cane with year of make in red, green, and blue encircling blue "J."

Jeannette Glass Company, 1898 to present. Jeannette, Pa.   C. 1940s made depression glass. Other table and gift wares. [AGR]

D. C. Jenkins Glass Co., Kokomo, Indiana. C. 1920s, maker of depression glass. [Florence]

    Sig.: molded

Jacques Gruber (1870–1938), France.   In 1897, left Daum to set up own shop. [Grover/Haida]

    Sig.: engraved on plaque with 5 acid cuttings.

    "Nancy" occasionally added.

Jacob Sang (active 1752, d. 1783), Amster-dam, Holland.   Diamond point engraver. [Weiss]

    Sig.: diamond point on upper side of goblet foot.

JACOB SANG FEC./
AMSTR AO 1763

Jacobus van den Blijk (1736–1814), Nether-lands.   Stipple engraver, copied contempo-rary paintings. [Weiss]

Signed work known

Jack Brewer, 20th century American. Designer. [Grover]

Sig.: engraved on base of free-form vase.

Jan Bot, 18th century, Netherlands. Engraver in diamond point. [Weiss]

Signed work known

Jan Cerny (b. 1907), Bohemia and Moravia, 20 years professor at Zelezny Brod. Designed glass sculptures and jewelry. [Grover]

JAN CERNY 1971
Also with title and date

M. V. Garnsey, Spring Lake & Grand Haven, Mich. Trade name active c. 1906. Glass figures and vases. [Peterson]

Sig.: molded

JAPANA

Jason. Believed to have been Syrian and to have worked in Italy during the first century A. D. making mold blown ware. [Newman]

JASON

Javit Badash, Hollis, N.Y. Trademark active 1970s. Table and gift ware. [G & T]

J. Thorpe and Company, N.Y. Retailer. [Auction]

Sig.: molded

JAYTHO

Etched on same piece: "R. Lalique"

John Bailey, American, early 1900s. Lamp-shade painter at Handel. [Grant]

    Sig.: scenic landscape painted on lamp shade by Handel.

                                                               J B

Jules Barbe, England. C. 1880s, decorated Queen's Burmese and cameo work at Thomas Webb & Sons, Dennis Glass works. [Newman/Manley]

                                                               J BARBE

Julius Bernstein & Co., London. Glass importers. Trademark registered 1885. [Manley]

John Choko, c. 1980s, Millville, N.J. Magnum paperweights. [Selman]

    Sig.: cane

    Sometimes date cane

I. Cayette, France. 19th century, designer for A. Walter. [Arwas]

John & Craig Ritchie, Wheeling, W. Va. Glass works established before 1829. Made plain, pressed, and art glass. [McKearin/Innes]

    Sig.: molded block capitals on pressed window pane c. 1831.

                                                J & C RITCHIE

Jean Cros, son of Henri Cros. France, working 1890s-1930. Worked in pâte de verre; after 1919 made glass panels. [Arwas]

Sig.: inscribed on a landscape panel of pâte de verre.

J CROS

Prof. Josef Drahoňovsky (b. 1877), Prague. Glass cutter, designed in the classical style. [Pazaurek]

Jean Descomps, France. Designer for A. Walter. [Arwas]

Sig.: pâte de verre, probably after 1919, also with title.

J)) A.W.N.

J. D. Ayckbown, Dublin, Ireland. [Davis]

Signature molded in base on decanters.

J D AYCKBOWN

Jean. Not further identified. Signed in cameo on French cameo vase, late 19th cen-turn. [Blount]

𝓙ean

Jean Beck (1862-1938), Germany. Working in Munich 1910-25. Designer. Operated studio for ceramics and glass wares. [Neuwirth]

Sig.: under the foot with acid stamp. Used on a vase of opaque milk-glass with overlay colorings and iridescence.

JEAN BECK
MÜNCHEN

Several other signatures noted.

JEAN BECK
MÜNCHEN

Jean Descomps, designer for A. Walter, Nancy, France, probably active 1920s. [Arwas]

Jean Descomps

Jean Sala (b. 1895), Paris, France. Blower and decorator. [Arwas]

    Sig.: on side or base in diamond point

Jean Sala

Jefferson Glass Company, Follansbee, W. Va. Early 20th century. Handpainted glass lamp shades.

    Sig.: usually fired on. Unfired thin lined script signatures are reported to be forgeries. [Cronin]

JEFFERSON GLASS CO.

Schott & Gen, Mainz, Germany. Trademark for domestic heat-resistant glass. Active c. 1970s. [EGD]

JENÄR GLAS

Jersey Glass Co., Jersey City. Established in 1824, became P. C. Dummer & Co. about 1830. C. 1827, began producing pressed glass. [McKearin]

    Sig.: molded in pressed glass salt dish.

JERSEY GLASS CO
NR N. YORK

Jewel Cut Glass Co., N.Y., N.Y. Cutting shop 1907-28 for brilliant cut glass. After 1928, continued operation as a gift shop. [JCK/Revi]

Johann F. Hoffmann (1840-1900), Carlsbad.
See: J. Hoffmann. [Weiss]   J. F. HOFFMANN

John Gentile, Gentile Glass Works, 20th
century, American. [Melvin]

   Sig.: collector edition paperweight   J G
   of George & Martha Washington. Dates
   refer to date first issued.

J. G. Farris, American. Signed on Wave
Crest ware box. [Auction]   J G FARRIS

J. Goy. Probably designer for Baccarat.

   Sig.: inscribed on crystal plaque   J. GOY
   of Mt. Rushmore.

   Also, with acid etched Baccarat trademark. [Auction]

See: Jacques Gruber. Signed on window   *J Gruben*

Joshua Hodgetts, late 19th c., England.   J. H.
 Worked with the Northwood team at Stevens
& Williams. Noted for rock-crystal style
engraving. [Grover]

Gentile Glass Works. Jimmy Hamilton per-
forms facet cutting on Gentile's collector
edition paperweights. [Melvin]

   Sig.: die marked   J H

Joseph Haberl (1800-1866), Vienna and
Neustadt. [Weiss]

J. HABERL 1821/W. NEUSTADT,
GESCHN VON

Johann Heinrich Balthasar Sang, Ilmenau/
Brunswick, Germany Court engraver at
Brunswick, working 1745-55. [Newman/Weiss]

J. H. B. SANG

J. H. Millstein Co., Jeannette, Pa. Twentieth century producer of commercial quality figurals.

   Sig.: relief molded on base in various
   sized block letters without serifs

J. H. MILLSTEIN CO. /
JEANNETTE, PA. /
PATENTED

MFG. BY J. H. MILLSTEIN CO. /
JEANNETTE. PA. -
PAT. APP. FOR

J. Hoare & Co., Corning, N.Y. C. 1853--
1920. Fine cut glass of the Brilliant
Period. Trademark registered in 1900,
but in use since 1895. [Revi/Boggess/-
Farrar]

   Sig.: 1895-1920 acid stamped.

Josef Hoffmann (1870-1955), Carlsbad, Czechoslovakia. Created style of decorating known as "Broncit" produced by Lobmeyr. Also, designed for Loetz and Moser. Was founder of Wiener Werkstätte. [Arwas]

Sig.: shallow engraved script on base of decorated vase. Possibly Moser period.

J. HOFFMANN

James M. Wayne (b. 1939), American. Sculptural vessels. In 1968, visiting instructor, at University of Southern California. [Grover]

JIM WAYNE 71

JIM WAYNE USC 1969

Josef Lanke, Steinschönau. Glass engraver. [Pazaurek]

JL

Joseph Locke. See monogram "J L." Cameo work. [Grover]

J L 1877

Johann Ludwig Faber (active 1678-1697), Nuremberg, Germany. Hausmaler in schwarzlot. Developed transparent enamels. [Weiss]

J. L. F. f.

J. & L. Lobmeyr, Vienna. Established 1823 in Bohemia. The Vienna branch became independent when the factory was nationalized in 1945. [Newman/Pazaurek]

Sig.: on edge of sulphide plaque.

J & L LOBMEYR WIEN

On same piece: paper label

PATENTED G S & CO

J. Lloyd, c. 1900, Stourbridge, England.
Engraved stemware.

    Sig.: one piece of each dozen was
    signed.

J. LLOYD

Jules Mabut, Paris. Luxurious art glass
shop. Sold works designed by Henri-
Alphonse Louis Laurent-Desrousseaux on
blanks from various makers, c. 1900.
[Blount/Arwas]

    Sig.: gilt

    Signed on base

A LA PAIX
J. MABUT
34 AVENUE de L'OPERA PARIS
MODELE DEPOSE

Verrerie de la Paix
Mabut

J. Michel, Paris, France, c. 1900, cameo
landscape vase. [Blount]

    Signed in cameo.

J. Michel
PARIS

Johann Josef Mildner (1764–1808), Gutenbrunn, Austria. Improved Zwichengoldglas
technique. [Newman]

J. MILDNER FEC/
À GUTENBRUNN 1796

J. Millward, artist at Stevens & Williams
during the 1940s. Revived cameo cutting
using old blanks from storage. [Grover/
Wakefield/Beard]

    Sig.: on cameo work.

J MILLWARD, STEVENS & WILLIAMS

J MILLWARD, 12, STEVENS & WILLIAMS

J MILLWARD, STEVENS & WILLIAMS LTD.,
BRIERLEY HILL

See: John Northwood.

    Sig.: on cameo plaques

J N

J N 880

J NORTHWOOD 1878

James Augustus Jobling, England. Active
c. 1920s, maker of pressed glass. [Antique
Collector]

    Sig.: molded in base. Also includes a
number.

JOBLING'S OPALIQUE

Joseph S. Barker (b. 1933), Newark, Dela-
ware. Maker of miniature paperweights.
[Melvin]

    Sig.: on paperweight cushion

JOE BARKER

Joel Philip Myers (b. 1934), American.
Director of design at Blenko Glass Co.
1960s. [Grover]

    Sig.: engraved. May include title.

JOEL PHILIP MYERS 1971

BLOWN BY JOEL PHILIP
MYERS AT BLENKO
1965

JOEL PHILIP MYERS 1971

Joh. Adam Wappler, active 1728, Nuremberg
and Dresden. Diamond point engraver.
[Weiss]

    Signed on a goblet.

JOH. ADAM WAPPLER
FECIT 1728

Rosenthal Glas & Porzellan A. G., Selb, Germany. Trade name active 1970s. May not have been used for glass. Seen on porcelain dinnerware. [EGD]

JOHANN HAVILAND

Johann Josef Mildner (1764-1808), Gutenbrunn, Austria. Improved the zwischengold glass technique. [Newman/Weiss]

Sig.: portrait in red and gold

JOHANN JOSEF MILDNER

Johann Kelly. Worked in schwarzlot and en grisaille. [Weiss]

Signed work known

Johannes Benedikt d. A Hess (1636-1674), Frankfurt, Germany. [Weiss]

JOH. BENED. HESS 1670

John E. Kemple Glass Works, Kenova, W. Va. Table and gift ware trademark active c. 1970s. [G & T]

John Heald Cook (b. 1942), England. Visiting designer at Venini c. 1968. Full time instructor at Leicester Polytechnic. [Grover]

JOHN H COOK LONDON 1968
EXHIBITED EXPO '70 OSAKA

See: Loetz

Sig.: paper label

JOHN LOETZ WITWE KLOSTERMUHLE

John Northwood (1836-1920), England. Developed numerous machines for working glass. Carved the "Pegasus" and the "Portland" vases. 1848, began work at Richardson's in Stourbridge; 1860, established J & J Northwood; 1881, technical advisor at Stevens & Williams; 1878, at Thos. Webb & Son. [Grover/Beard]

JOHN NORTHWOOD

JOHN NORTHWOOD 1878

John Northwood II (1870-1960), son of John Northwood. Worked in cameo. [Beard/ Grover]

    Sig.: in cameo

JOHN NORTHWOOD II

John Schaper (1621-70), Nüremberg, Germany. Schwarzlot painting of landscape and battle scenes. Invented some new transparent enamel colors for glass painting. [Weiss]

    Sig.: on beaker with schwarzlot painting of combat scene.

JOHN SCHAPER 1665

John Gundersen, Norway. Active 1970s. Glass sculpture. Worked at Hadelands Tradeschool. [Grover]

JOHN GUNDERSEN /
NORWAY HADELANDS F S

Josair. Limited edition plates beginning c. 1972. [Kovel]

Believed to be signed

Graf Schaffgotsch'sche Josephinenhütte GmbH, Ger. Trade name active c. 1970s, used on 24% lead crystal wares. [EGD/Bröhan]

Sig.: paper label of silver with blind stamp; applied to Art Deco design perfume bottle

See: Joseph Locke under "JL" monogram.   JOSEPH LOCKE 1878

J. P. Imberton, Paris, circa 1890.

Sig.: on base of enameled beaker

John Gentile, Gentile Glass Works. Twentieth century, American.

Sig.: on paperweight   J R G 1959

Stourbridge Flint Glass Works, 1823-1835, Pittsburgh, Pa. Glass works established by John Robinson. [Innes]

Sig.: molded in lacy pressed salt dish   J ROBINSON & SON / PITTSBURGH

Jean Sala (b. 1895). Blower and decorator in his own shop on Paris Left Bank. Worked with coarse impure bubbly glass. Noted for "Sala" blue. Worked with his father, Bienvenu. See index for other signatures. [Arwas]

Sig.: on base or side engraved with diamond point.

Jules-Paul Brateau, France. In 1910, began experiments with pâte de verre. Used floral motifs in pastel colors. See device for "B. Jules." [Grover]

JULES BRATEAU

Justrite Mfg. Co., Chicago, Ill. Trademark active c. 1911, acid stamp on lighting wares. [Peterson]

JustRite

J. Viard, France. Early 1900s. [Auction]

Sig.: used on a powder box of industrial quality with molded and stained decorative treatment. Name molded in bottom and also acid etched in lid with smeared block letters.

J VIARD /
MADE IN FRANCE

Jacob Weber (1637-1685), Switzerland. Glass painter. [Gessert]

j·Weber

J. W. Not further identified. Silesia c. 1730s. Used on a beaker with intaglio engraving. [Weiss]

J. W. SILESIA

K

Krantz, Smith & Co. and
Krantz & Sell Co. (successors), Honesdale,
Pa. Established 1893, in operation until
early 1920s. Cutting shop for brilliant cut
glass. [Revi]

Charles Kaziun, Brockton, Mass. Paperweights of millefiori designs and florals,
w/gold foil inclusions; perfume bottle
weights, footed miniatures, buttons.
[Selman/Cloak]

 Sig.: gold on base and/or Millefiori
cane seen from back.

K

F. Kretschmann, England. Cameo worker at
Webb. [Grover]

K

Vineland Flint Glass Works, Vineland, N. J.
Established in 1897 by Victor Durand, Jr.,
who was inspired by Louis C. Tiffany.

 Sig.: engraved and silvered on bottom
of vessels. "K" designates Cluthra
glass; Dec., decoration; single digit
number, the color; four digit number,
stock number; last single digit number,
size.

1812~,
K
Dee. 32

Kimble Glass Co., Vineland, N.J. Owned by
Evan F. Kimble. C. 1931 acquired Vineland
Flint Glass Works after Durand's death.

 Trademark c. 1920

 Used after 1936

K

K

190

C. Koepping (1896-1900). German Art Nouveau designer of delicate long stemmed
wares. [Arwas]

    Sig.: vessel engraved underfoot and
"Koepping" on side

Leonard Krower, New Orleans, La. Brilliant
style cut glass. Probably a jobber. [JCK]

    Trademark active c. 1915.

Koloman Moser (1868-1918), Austrian. Member of the Wiener Werkstätte. Designer for
Loetz. [Schweiser]

    Sig.:

Kaj Franck (b. 1911), Finland. Designer at
Oy Wartsila, Notsjoe, c. 1950s-70s. Became
Art Director in 1970s. Sculptural vessels.
[Grover]

KAJ FRANCK NUUTAJARVI
NOTSJO

Karhula. Used on a cordial glass with
enamel decoration, c. 1870. Probably
Finish. Not further identified. [On exhibit at Corning]

KARHULA

Karl Massanetz (1890–1918), Steinschönau, Czechoslovakia. [Neuwirth]

Signed on a pokal of crystal with black feather drawing and gold decoration, c. 1912. Signature located inside cover of dome.

Kaza. France, early 20th century. Used on an Art Deco design vase of clear and frosted glass. [Auction]

Sig.: inscribed

KAZA PARIS

Katherine Casey, American, early 20th century.   Lamp shade painter at Handel. [Grant]

Sig.: painted or scratched

KC

K CASEY

Keith Richard Cummings (b. 1940), London, England. Worked at Whitefriars & taught at Stourbridge College of Art. Specialized in flat glass sculpture and architectural designs. [Grover]

KEITH CUMMINGS
also w/date

Keith Murray.   In 1932, began as designer for Stevens & Williams, England. Worked for them until 1939. [Stevens & Williams/ Polak]

Sig.:   name engraved; "Brierley" acid etched stencil

Keith Murray
BRIERLEY

C. F. Monroe Co., Meriden Conn. Trade name registered c. 1904 for decorated opal glass ware. Also listed for brilliant cut glass. [Grimmer]

Sig.: printed in pink on opal wares

TRADE KELVA MARK

Kent F. Ipsen, (b. 1933) USA. Teacher of glass making. [Grover]

KENT F IPSEN 1972

Valdimir Kepka (b. 1925) & Zdenek Kepka, brothers from Czechoslovakia. Designers of sculptural forms. [Grover]

KEPKA 1971
w/title

Thomas Manufacturing Co., Dayton, Ohio. Trade name registered c. 1913 for lighting. [Peterson]

KEROSAFE

Union Glass Co., (c. 1851-1924), Sommerville, Mass. Trade name registered c. 1853 is an anagram of William S. Blake, the founder. Used on small iridescent lamp shades. [Roberts]

Sig.: engraved

Acid etched signatures are not authentic.

KEW-BLAS

Macbeth-Evans Glass Co., Pittsburgh, Pa. C. 1890, etched on high quality lead glass, of the same quality as their "Zenith" but specially packed in corrugated tubes or in hay. [Catalouge]

193

H. M. Rio Co., Philadelphia, c. 1890s. Decorated opal ware, similar to "Wavecrest." [Revi]

KEYSTONE WARE

See: "KK" for Kunst und Kunsthandwerke, Fachschule, Haida, Bohemia. [Neuwirth]

Sig.: engraved on crystal vase with cut and enamel decorative treatment.

Also used as a paper label.

KHK

Kaj Franck, from 1951, Art Director at Notsjö Glassworks, Nuutajärvi, Finland. [Polak]

K. Franck.
Nuutajärvi
Notsjö -59

K. Hable, Carlsbad, Czechoslovakia. Active 1970s. Engraver of vases, glass plaques, etc. for Ludwig Moser's Glass Works. [Auction]

Sig.: may also include title.

K HABLE 1979 /
MOSER CARLSBAD

Georg Friedrich Killinger (died 1726), active c. 1694. Diamond point engraver; later turned to wheel engraving. [Weiss]

Sig.: used on covered goblet.

KILLINGER FEC. NORIB

Division of Owens-Illinois, Toledo, Ohio. Trade name active. c. 1970s. [AGR]

KIMBLE

194

Kingsbridge, Bavaria, Germany. Limited edition crystal decanters and plates, each piece hand-engraved with duck designs, numbered, and signed. [Kovel]

Believed to be signed

George L. Borden & Co., Krystal Krafters, Trenton and Groveville, N. J. Cut glass. Trademark. [Revi]

Kunst und Kunstgewerbe Staatsfachschule, Steinschönau, Czechoslovakia. [Pazaurek]

Sig.: older mark wheel engraved. Used on cameo vase.

K. K. F. S. ST.

later marks:

KK $ ST

See: "KK" for Kunst und Kunsthandwerke, Fachschule, Haida, Bohemia. [Neuwirth]

K·K·
FACHSCH·HAIDA·

Karl Lorenz, c. 1909, teacher of engraving at Fachschule in Steinschönau and Haida, Czechoslovakia. [Neuwirth]

K L

Charles F. A. Hinrichs, N.Y., N.Y. Agent for Kleeman of Erfurt, Prussia, German Student Lamps. Trade name registered c. 1863. [Peterson]

KLEEMANN

Miroslav Klinger (b. 1922), Czechoslovakia. Since 1948 designer of figurines at Zeleznobrodske, Czechoslovakia. [Grover]

KLINGER 1971
also w/title

Crystal Glass Co, Bagley & Co. Ltd., England Trademark for pressed ware, active c. 1970s. [EGD]

KNOTTINGLEY CRYSTAL

KNOTTINGLEY CRYSTALTYNT

Edward J. Koch & Co., Elgin, Ill., c. 1899-1925. Made some fine brilliant cut glass, but trade name used on pressed blanks for cut glass. [Revi]

Köck not identified. [Novy Bor]

    Signed on cameo vase.

Carl Koepping, (1848-1914), Berlin. Designed Jugendstil tall stemmed thinly blown drinking glasses. [Arwas/Hilschenz]

    Sig.: engraved under base

Richard Murr, San Francisco, Calif. Trade name registered 1905; not active in 1915. Label used on pressed blanks for cut glass. Also cut some fine glass designs. [Revi/ JCK]

KOH-I-NOOR

Kosta, oldest continually worked glass factory and leading contemporary Swedish

glass maker. Founded in 1742 by Andres
Koskull and Georg Bogislaus Stael von
Holstein. Named from the first letters of
founders' names. [Newman/Arwas]

Current trademark.

Sig.: cameo vase

Sig.: engraved on intaglio cut, Art Deco
vase. Elis Bergh (1881-1954) designer
at Kosta from 1927.

KOSTA B-W 86 BERGH

Came. Designer. Signed on vase with
molded and etched decoration.

KOSTA 1936 CAME 16/2315

Vicke Lindstrand (b. 1904). Designer.
Came to Kosta from Orrefors in 1950 to
become director of design.

KOSTA LINDSTRAND 1970

KOSTA 59 TIL KARIN/
VICKE LINDSTRAND

Engraved. Mona Morales-Schildt, designer at Kosta since 1958.

KOSTA 1969 /
MONA MORALES-SCHILDT /
5-423

Engraved. Rolf Sinnemark, designer at
Kosta since 1967.

KOSTA-UNIK R SINNEMARK

Probably designed by Lindstrand; "H"
denoting hand work; signed in diamond
point

Designer not identified

Kosta

K

Circa 1950's, possibly designed by Lindstrand; "U" denoting fire polishing.

KOSTA LU 2100

Ann Schaefer Warff (b. 1937), wife of Goran Warff (b. 1933). Designers at Kosta since 1964.

KOSTA-UNIK 692 ANN
AND GORAN WARFF 1969

C. 1970 introduced limited edition mugs, plates, paperweights; c. 1976 limited edition sculptures.

Kruh, Prague, c. 1920. [Novy Bor]

Benjamin Edwin Foster, Surrey, England. Decorator of glass wares. Trade name registered 1885. [Manley]

KRUSTALLOS

Ohio Flint Glass Co., c. 1900-08; Jefferson Glass Co., 1908-18; Central Glass Works, c. 1919. [Cat./Kovel]

    Trade name with design patent date molded in clear glass creamer and sugar

PATENTED
Krys-Tol
FEB. 5, 1907

K. Schaffer, Bohemia [Blount]

    Sig.: in enamel on covered box with cameo and enamel decoration.

K SCHAFFER
Bohemia

Karl Schmoll von Eisenwerth, glass designer at Munich and Stuttgart in the Art
Deco style. [Exhibition]

    Sig.: diamond point in pontil; used only
    on unique pieces

KSᵛE

Attributed to Steuben Glass Works, Corning,
New York, circa 1930. [Auction]

    Sig.: molded in plaque with medium
    relief profile

KT / H

Georg Gottlieb Kuhnt (1805-85), Breslau,
Bohemia. Glass mosaic panels with scenes
of spas. [Newman]

Signed work known.

Frank Kulasiewicz, USA. Taught glass
making, and in 1964, opened his own glass
studio. Developed an original glass formula. [Grover]

    Sig.: may include date and title

KULASIEWICZ

Col. Evan F. Kimble and Conrad Vahlsing.
Reported as a forgery on iridescent ware
similar to those produced by Durand, Steuben or Quezal in the early 20th century.
[Cronin]

K - V

See: "K Casey." Katherine Casey Welch.
Lamp shade painted for Handel. [Grant]

K WELCH

Karl Wiedmann (1905-1970), West Germany.
In 1927, became works manager at WMF.
Following World War II was technical mana-
ger at Daum et Cie until 1947. Head of
glass department at WMF 1948-51. Head of
Farberglaswerke at Zwiesel. Technical
director of Gral Glas 1954-70. [Newman/
Schwandt]

Sig.: diamond point

K WIEDMANN 1971 /
GRAL-GLAS DURNAU

L

J & L Lobmeyr, Bohemia and Vienna, Austria. C. 1860 to present. Moved to Austria when nationalized in 1945. Fine quality glass, cut, engraved, iridescent, Art Nouveau and classical designs. [Arwas]

   Sig.: engraved or painted, used after 1860.

Lotte Baar (b. 1901), Breslau. Glass engraver. [Pazaurek]

See: Libbey. [Faustus]

   Sig.: registered c. 1937; used after 1962 for domestic wares

   c. 1955, heat treated tumblers: "'L' blown in," star etched. number to left: year of make; number to right, quarter of year of make.

Chris Lebeau (1878-1945), At Leerdam from 1924-25, designer for "Unika" art glass and flower vases. Free-lance worker. [Leerdam]

Floris Meydam (1919-). Designer at
Leerdam. Each piece after his design
marked "Unika" with number and date letter.

C. C. van Asch - van Wijck (1900-32), Leerdam. From 1929 free lance designer for
glass sculptures. [Leerdam/Arwas]

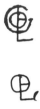

K. P. C. de Bazel (1869-1923). Architect.
C. 1916-21 designer at Leerdam for table
and drink wares, vases, annual beakers,
pressed glass. [Leerdam/Arwas]

Sig.: 1916-23

C. 1922-45

Sandblasted ware c. 1946/47

Lucienne Bloch. Active circa 1900 to 1905
at Leerdam. Designer of wall paintings and
tapestries. Designed satin glass animal
figures. [Leerdam]

Cornelis de Lorm (1875-1942), Leerdam.
From 1916 to 1925, free lance designer for
drink wares, painted objects, artistic cut
glass, and domestic ware. [Leerdam/Arwas]

Andries Dirk Copier (b. 1901). Came to
Leerdam in 1914; from 1923-67, art director
for Unika art glass. Developed and produced Gilde-Glas, which until about 1950
carried the mark of the Vereniging Neder-
landsche Wijnhandelaars (V.N.W. for Associated Wine Distributors). [Leerdam/
Arwas/Van der Meer]

Sig.: 1923-45, diamond point on base

Sandblasted, c, 1946-47

"Gildglas" made for the Vereniging Neder-
landsche Wijnhandelaars

Ida Falkenberg-Liefrinck, Leerdam. Architect. For a short time in the late
1930s, free lance designer for vases and
production glass. [Leerdam/Van der Meer]

William Heesen (b. 1925) Started at
Leerdam in 1943. Signed each piece of
"Unica" glass made after his design with
number and date letter. [Pazaurek]

Christiaan Johannes Lanooy (1881-1948),
Leerdam. Potter. Designer for production
glass from 1919 to 1930; for Unika vessels
from 1925 to 1929. [Leerdam]

Frits Lensfeld (1886-1945), Leerdam. Interior designer. C. 1926-30 designer for lamps. [Leerdam]

Joep Nicolas (1897-1972), Leerdam. Glass painter. End of 1930s up to 1945, free lance designer of vases. [Leerdam]

Jules Vermeire (b. 1885), Leerdam. C. 1930-32 free lance designer for animal figures. [Leerdam]

Lackawanna Cut Glass Co., Scranton, Pa. Active 1903-05, mail order business for brilliant cut glass. [Boggess]

 Sig.: etched on carafe and tumbler

Vicke Lindstrand, designer at Orrefors Glass Works, c. 1928-41. [Newman]

 "A" used to denote hand-cut glass work at Orrefors, "L" for Lindstrand.   LA

 "U" denotes fire polish   LU

See: "Legras"

 Sig.: gilt on overlay glass with acid cuttings. Art Nouveau vessels often with red interior, gilt signature

E. De La Chapelle & A. M. Paturle, Brooklyn, N.Y. Trade name for numerous types of
glassware from 1876. C. 1915 acquired by
Macbeth-Evans for use on lamp chimneys and
globes. [Peterson]

    Sig.: Etched or impressed.

LA BASTIE

Dominick Labino, Grand Rapids, Ohio.
Paperweights and art glass. [Cloak]

    Sig.: inscribed on underside.

*L abino
1 9 6 8*

Lazarus & Rosenfeld, end of the 19th century. Importers of pseudo-cameo work,
painted with opaque enamels in floral and
lace designs on colored satin body. [Revi]

    Sig.: printed block letters etched on
bottom of vase.

LAC-DE-BOHEME CAMEO

L. Adams, Holland. Working in 1806.
Stipple engraver. [Newman]

Signed work known

See: R. Lalique. [Novy Bor/Arwas/Bley]

    Sig.: engraved plus reversed monogram:
"K M," attributed to Kolo Moser. Used
on a vase molded with a group of
swallows.

Lalique

Impressed

[ALIQUE]

Acid etched on mold blown colored finger bowl and on frosted molded bowl made after factory reopened after World War II under direction of Lalique's son, Marc

cristal
LALIQUE
France

Contemporary

Lalique france

See: Loetz. Engraved in cameo on a cameo vase. [Blount]

La Loetz

Lamartine. Probably France. Not further identified. [Whitlow/Novy Bor]

Sig.: intaglio carved vase

LAMARTINE 327 / 610

On a cameo vase with scenic design.

Lamartine

Lamb Studios, New York. Nineteenth century stained glass window studio.

Sig.: painted on leaded glass window.

LAMB Studios
N.Y.

Lansburgh & Brother, Washington, D. C. Brilliant period glass cutting shop. [Revi]

Trademark for commercial quality vases and crystal.

LANSBURGH & BRO.

Cristallerie et Verrerie de Vianne, France. Trade name. [ANV]

LANTERNES

La Zover. (Or La Royer) Not further identified. [Auction]

    Sig.: inscribed on a vase decorated in an Art Deco style.

LA ROYER

S. F. Myers Co., N.Y., N.Y. Wholesale and retail outlet and cutting shop for brilliant cut glass. Trade name inactive by 1915. [JCK]

LAUREL

Laurel Cut Glass Company, Jermyn, Penna. Name used from 1907 to 1920. [Boggess]

    Sig.: acid etched on a plate.

Laurens Glass, Indian Head Inc., Laurens, S. C. Trademark active 1970s

Lautum. France. C. 1930s. Not further identified.

    Sig.: inscribed on lampshade with painted scenic design. [Auction]

LAUTUM

La Zoyer, France. Used on Art Deco cordial glasses and plates. See above: La Rover (?). [Auction]

LA ZOYER

LA ZOYER, FRANCE

Louis Comfort Tiffany.   See: Louis C.
Tiffany. [McKean]

3965 M L.C.T. - Favrile

Sig.: Engraved on base near edge. Never
acid etched.

These signatures are usually engraved on
edge, but also known in pontil. When
acid etched, it is a forgery. Only the
rare monogram signature was ever acid
etched.

After 1902, may be wheel cut block
letters.
Used on rock crystal vase

115 L.C.TIFFANY

Glass tile: embossed on back

PAT. FEB. 8TH 1881
L.C.T. & Co.

On same tile, obverse, engraved

SAMPLE H 1

On polished flat surface of either side
of small blown lamp shade fitter rim,
signature may include number and prefix,
an "O" for special order, or "L," "M,"
or "S" on small shades. [Roberts]

Used on a Favrile vase

1525-4804 M-L.C. Tiffany Inc. Favrile

"O" symbol used as a prefix to indicate
special order.

Ɵ 127

"X" used as a prefix to indicate
experimental work.

$$X 87 \cdot 3965 \text{ M } L.C.Y. \text{ Favrile}$$

"EX" denoted "Exhibition piece."   "EX" preceeding number and
                                                signature

Other exhibition piece signatures: L. C. TIFFANY FAVRILE EXHIBITION
                                               PIECE 256

                                               L. C. TIFFANY / D 752 /
                                               SAN FRANCISCO

"A-Col" used on pieces from Tiffany's
personal collection

$$62 A-coll. \, L.C.y\text{iffany}$$

Used on a goblet designed and decorated   L.C.T. FAVRILE
by A. J. Nash, from the A. J. and L. H.   A.J.N.
Nash collection.

Engraved, from the A. J. and L. H. Nash
collection   L.C.T. FAVRILE
                                               A. J. NASH

L.C.T. engraved; the other in enamel.
From the A. J. and L. H. Nash Collec-   L. C. TIFFANY /
tion.   A. J. NASH

Louis Damon (d. 1947), France. In 1887, opened an independent decorating shop, commissioned blanks from Daum. Produced deep wheel carved intaglio floral and plant motifs, mythological figures. [Arwas]

Sig.: incised in script on base.

Damon

Paris

Damon

L Damon
20 B⁰ᵛ Malesherbes
Paris

Lederle Studios, 20th century. Used on stained glass landscape window. [Auction]

LEDERLE STUDIOS

Ledoux, c. 1920s.

Signed in cameo on cameo vase.

LEDOUX

Leerdam, Netherlands glass works, founded 1765 to make cheap housewares and bottles. C. 1915 began to employ artist-designers. Copier introduced heavy blown crystal. C. 1925, Hendrick P. Berlage established the "Unica" studio for art glass. [Newman/Arwas/Van der Meer]

Trademark in use since 1928

Sig.: Diamond point on pieces of "unique" or individual design

„LEERDAM UNICA"
H37

Date letters used on "Unica" wares:

1926-27	A
1927	B
1927-28	C
1928	D
1928-29	E
1929-30	F
1930-31	G, H
1931-32	K, L, M
1932	N
1933-34	O & #'s 1-200
1935-36	O & #'s 200-300
1937	O & #'s 300-400
1938	O & #'s 400-662
1939	P
1940	R
1941	S
1942	T
1943	V
1944	W
1946	X
1947	Z

and continuing with double letters

Sig.: designed by Floris Meydam, at Leerdam from 1935. This signature believed to date c. 1950s.

LEERDAM UNICA M D 737
LL F MEYDAM

Sybren Valkema, designer. Signature engraved on a vase, circa 1966.

R. Strebelle, designer circa 1926-27; signed in diamond point [Van der Meer]

R Strebelle
„LEERDAM UNICA"
A 37

Etched marks used until 1949, after that sandblasted

See monograms at front of "L" section for other designers.

Andries Dirk Copier, at Leerdam from 1914 to 1967; diamond point in pontil

„LEERDAM-UNICA"
V.969
A D Copier

Christiaan Johannes Lanooy, from 1919 to 1929/30 at Leerdam

„LEERDAM UNICA
C J Lanooy
E 209

Chris Lebeau, at Leerdam from 1924 to 1925

LEERDAM UNICA
278
CHRIS- LE-BEAU
-OCT- 1925-

Legras, in 1864, established by August J. F. Legras at St Denis, France. Merged with Pantin after World War I. Also see: Mt.

Mont Joye & Cie. Produced intaglio, cameo, or pseudo-cameo designs with enamels. Landscape and floral subjects were popular. [Blount/Arwas]

    Sig.: acid cut cameo design and signature, sometimes with enhancement

Legras   (a)

Iegras   (b)

    After 1918, signed in paint on side of a vase from their commercial line of enamel painted vessels

Leg   (a)

Legras   (b)

    See: Mont Joye
(a) Usually vessel with transparent body and frosted surface with gilt and enamel: Engraved on side of vessel

legras   (a)

(b) In gilt under foot of same vessel

Mont Joye Luce (logo)   (b)

L'Elf. No further identification.

    Signed in cameo on a cameo vase. [Whitlow]

L'ELF

Société Française de Verrerie Mecanique Champenoise, Reims, France. Trade name. [ANV]

LE MEILLEUR

Lencx Crystal Inc., Mt Pleasant, Pa.   20th
century. Stem and gift wares. [T&G]

Société Française de Verrerie Mecanique
Champensoise, France. Trade name. [ANV]

LE PARFAIT-SUPER

Leune. Not further identified.

    Sig: in enamel on enamel decorated
vases. [Auction]

Possibly Le Verre Français.   Signed under
foot of three color cameo vase and worked
into cameo design. [Auction]

Le Verre Français. See: Schneider.
[Blount/Arwas]

    Sig.: engraved on side or on upper foot
in a variety of styles. Used on cameo
work.

Retailer on Bond Street, London, that
commissioned special work

FINNIGANS

John Conrad Lewis (b. 1942), USA. Sculptor, made many styles of "moon bottles." [Grover]

LEWIS 1971/with Title

Liberty Glass Co., Sapula, Okla. Trademark active 1970s. [AGR]

LG

L. G. Wright Glass Co., New Martinsville, W. Va. Table and gift ware. Trademark active 1970s. [T&G]

Label

Molded in reverse on bottom of reproduction opalescent cranberry swirl bottle

L.G.WRIGHT

Henri A. Copillet, glass works established 1890s; destroyed during World War II. Produced dark metallic iridescent glass. [Arwas]

Sig.: stenciled in script capitals

H.COPILLET

On same vase, worked into the decoration Translated: "The man, the metal worker"

LHOMME LEFEVRE

W. L. Libbey & Son, Toledo, Ohio. Established 1893; presently operating as division of Ownes-Illinois. Makers of fine glassware. Made brilliant cut wares of fine quality during late 19th century, later used molded blanks. Produced Amberina, Pomona, Maize, Peachblow, and other art glass. [Fauster/Boggess]

Sig.: used on Amberina ware made after 1917

Used 1892-1896, paper label or printed in light brownish red on souvenirs between 1892 and 1896 for the Columbian Exposition on items decorated by the Smith Brothers.

1896-1906 etched on cut glass

1896-1906 cut and engraved glass, label or etched.

1906-1913 etched on cut glass and light globes

1919-1930

1933-1935

1924/39-1945

1959-1968

Act. 1970s

LIBBEY GLASS

Forgeries of the etched marks have been reported. Be sure to check for size, detail, clarity, quality of object and signature.

Stanislav Libensky (b. 1921), glass teacher, husband of Jaroslava Brychtova Libensky (b. 1921), Czechoslovakia. Sculptors. [Grover]

LIBENSKY-BRYCHTOVA
w/title and date

Liberty Cut Glass Works, Egg Harbor City, N. J. C. 1902-32, cutting shop for brilliant cut glass. [JCK/Revi]

See: Imperial Glass Co. "LIG:" last Imperial glass. Last day's run, after factory was sold in 1980s. Used on Cambridge Glass Co. Dresden dolls, Heisey dolls, and an Imperial bell. [Warman]

   Sig.: molded

L.I.G.

Lily Division of Owens-Illinois, Toledo, Ohio. Trademark active 1970s. [AGR]

LILY
OI

Linden Glass Co. (1888-1909) and
Linden Co. (1910-1934). Chicago. Produced
leaded windows, glass mosaics, and lighting
fixtures. [Darling]

Lin JEN C°

Marvin Lipofsky (b. 1938), USA. One of
first to break from traditional glass
forms. Worked with Harvey Littleton.
Sculptor. [Grover]

LIPOFSKY 1966-67

Ladislav Jezek (b. 1930), Czechoslovakia.
Since 1957 worked at government works of
Zeleznobrodske Sklo at Zelezny, Brod.
Engraver and designer. [Grover]

L. JEZEK-MENCL 1970
w/title

French paperweight. Not further identified. [Cloak]

   Sig.: impressed on underside of paperweight.

LL PARIS MADE IN FRANCE

Louis Majorelle (1859-1926), France. Designer of the Nancy Art Nouveau school.
Designed for Daum Glass Works from 1918 to
1925, chiefly metal mounts, but also glass
ware.

   Sig.: under foot of vessel; also signed
   "Daum."

L. majorelle

Moser Glass Works, Karlsbad, Czechoslovakia. Ludwig Moser (1833-1916), Karlsbad.
Cameo on crystal. [Grover]

L M K MOSER KARLSBAD

Leslie Nash bogus signature used on Tiffany style wares. [Cronin]

Sig.: script

L. NASH /
LIBBEY—OWENS CO.

Joseph Locke & Sons, succeeded by Locke Art Glassware Co., Mount Oliver, Pa. Joseph Locke (1846-1936) established his own shop after 1891. Was formerly designer, enameler, and creator of new types of art glass for Libbey. (Newman/Revi]

Trademark for cut glass of the brilliant period, active c. 1915.

Worked into the design

H. V. Lockhorst, 18th century, Netherlands. Engraver in diamond point. [Weiss]

Signed work known

Lötz (or Anglicized: Loetz). Glass factory established 1836, Klostermühel, Bohemia by Eisenstein. Purchased in 1840, by Johann Loetz (1778-1848). Continued as "Johann Loetz Witwe" (Loetz's widow) after his death. Patented formula for iridescent glass in 1890. Made other art glass types in the Art Nouveau style. [Neuwirth/Arwas]

Sig.: wheel cut

Used after 1891 for export to the United States. Wheel cut.

Cameo with swirling tail representing a "C" and underlining the name, used on commercial grade ware after 1911.

Loetz

Inscribed in gilt on base. Milla Weltmann, designer, exhibited for Loetz in 1914 at the Cologne Crafts Alliance Exhibition.

MILLA WELTMANN LOETZ.

Circle usually acid etched in pontil, "Loetz" wheel engraved

Loetz

Architect Arnold Nechansky, designer c. 1914.

LOETZ BEZ.
ARCH. NECHANSKY

Dagobert Pèche, designer, c. 1914.

ARCH. D. PECHE

Kolo Moser, designer, c. 1901. Vase of opaque iridescent glass.

Max von Spaun, nephew of Loetz, manager and designer from 1870.

Spaun.

Verreries d'Art Lorraine (Verrerie de Belle Étoile), France. 20th c. Lighting fixtures and other art glass. [Catalogue/Blount/Venzmer]

Glass and wrought iron vase, c. 1930s. [Auction]. Sig.: inscribed. Lorraine glass and New York retailer.

Vase of cased glass with multi-colored enamel. Sig.: cameo on foot

C. Dorflinger & Sons, White Mills, Pa. Trade name c. 1894 for cut glass. [Peterson]

LORRAINE

Lorraines, enamelled vase c. 1910. [Blount]

See: D. Christian. Cameo vase.

LOTH
w/date

David Lotton (b. 1935), USA. Floral paperweights, vases. [Selman/Grover]

Sig.; incised on base of vessel or on base w/date and edition number of paperweight.

Lotus Cut Glass Co., Barnesville, Ohio. Trademark c. 1911, for cut glass. Still active c. 1970s for gift wares. [T&G]

Lötz. See: Loetz

Louie Glass Co., Weston, W. Va. Trademark
active c. 1970s, table and gift wares.
[T&G]

Louis Comfort Tiffany, Tiffany Studios, New
York. See Tiffany. [McKean/Auctions]

Sig.: engraved on a paperweight   LOUIS C. TIFFANY FAVRILE
from the Nash Collection.   EX 1274 LHN PARIS GOLD METAL

In enamel on the same vase: L. C. TIFFANY FAVRILE/L.H. NASH

Engraved script on vase, after 1902.

Louis C. Tiffany Furnaces Inc. Favrile

Windows for commercial purposes:

Early pieces with red or black enamel or
Later, acid etched,

Generally in the lower right on piece of
flashed glass with signature in resist,
the glass leaded into the design

Block letters on leaded windows, attributed to having been made after 1902.

Louis C. Tiffany

Other signatures: see "Tiffany" and "L.
C. T."

Lowell Cut Glass Co., Lowell, Mass. Cutting shop of brilliant cut glass, early 1900s. [Revi/Daniels]

Verrerie d'Arte, Loÿs Lucha. Signed on a multi-colored stained pressed glass suspension shade with relief cutting, c. 1930s. European. Suspension lighting globes. [Catalogue/Uecker]

Livio Seguso, Murano, Italy. Glass sculptor, active circa 1970s-80s.

Lloyd & Summerfield, Park Glass Works, Birmingham, Eng. Glass manufacturers for all type glasswares. Trademark registered 1877. [Manley]

Ludvika Smĕkova (b. 1903), designer for Glashütte Nižbor.

    Sig.: diamond point on drink service

Lewis & Towers, London. Glass manufacturer. Trademark registered 1910. [Manley]

Lubomir Richter, Corning, N. Y. Engraver
c. 1970s. [Farrar]

LUBOMIR RICHTER

Jefferson Glass Co., Follansbee, W. Va.
Trade name circa 1910. Lighting wares.
[Peterson]

LUCEO

Luciano Ferro, designer, c. 1950s. Vase
with color inlay. [Auction]

LUCIANO FERRO 1952

William H. Lum, succeeded by William H. Lum
& Son, N.Y., N.Y. Cutting shop for
brilliant cut glass. Trademark active
c. 1915. [JCK]

Webb and Corbett, England. Early 1900s.
Applied decorations on a vase. [Wilkinson/
Arwas]

   Sig. Ludwig Kny, designer

LU KNY

Lundberg Studios, established 1970 by James
Lundberg (b. 1948), California. Revival of
Art Nouveau styles using heat reactive
metallic oxides. Makes a wide range of
Tiffany-style vases, paperweights with as-
tronomical designs, birds, flowers, butterflies. [Selman]

Lundberg

   Sig.: Vases

LUNDBERG-5/20/1972

   Paperweights

LUNDBERG STUDIOS
plus date, artist's
name, & edition serial
number

224

Some glass has Lundberg's name ground away and a Tiffany signature added. Check iridescence, glass, etc.

Luscher. Not further identified. [Blount]

    Sig.: in cameo on cameo vase.

R. E. Tongue & Bros., Philadelphia, Pa. C. 1894, lighting wares trade name. [Peterson]

LUSTRE

Lustre Art Glass Co., Maspeth, Long Island, N.Y. Established c. 1920 by Conrad Vahlsing. Maker of small iridescent lamp shades, some vases and bowls. [Roberts]

    Sig.: engraved inside fitter rim of small shades on edge closest to viewer.

Not authentic [Cronin]

LUSTRE ART CO.

Per Lütken (b. 1916) Denmark. In 1942, chief designer at Holmegaard. Name and date signed on each piece made after his designs. [Newman/Polak]

LÜTKEN

Luzerne Cut Glass Co., Pittston, Pa. Cutting shop for brilliant cut glass. Trademark active in 1915 until 1930. [JCK/Revi]

Louis F. Vaupel. Engraver at Libbey c. 1875-80. [Fauster]

Sig.: under foot on mercury glass chalice, circa 1865-70.

L V

Lawrence Whistler (b. 1912), England Independent glass engraver in stipple and diamond point. Began working in 1935 with diamond point, later used carborundum. Early work is inscriptions and emblems; later period: architectural and pictorial. Some pieces are engraved both inside and outside. [Newman]

Sig.: on recent work often with date

Lyons Cut Glass Co., Lyons, N.Y. Cutting shop for brilliant cut glass, trademark active c. 1903-1915. [Revi/Daniels]

M

C. F. Monroe, Meriden, Conn. Fine cut
glass, mold blown decorated opal ware.
Closed in 1916. Trademark. [Revi]

M. de Meyer, designer at Maastricht,
Holland. Working about 1928. [van der
Meer]

McKanna Cut Glass Co., Honesdale, Pa.,
active 1914-1927. Cutting shop for brilliant cut glass. [JCK/Revi]

   Trademark

Maria Kirschner, Prague. Circa 1903 active
as designer for Loetz. [Pazaurek/Arwas]

   Sig.: under foot of vase.

Koloman Moser (1868-1918), Bohemia. Member
of Vienna Secession and Wiener Werkstätte.
[Arwas]

   Sig.: iridescent vase
   also signed "Loetz"

Ludwig Moser & Sons, Karlsbad, Czechoslovakia. Founded by Ludwig Moser (1833-
1916). Still in business. [Arwas]

Signature attributed to Moser, Karlsbad.

Same piece signed with unidentified
designer's monogram, possibly a designer
of the Wiener Werkstätte.

Marie Elizabeth John (b. 1903), Breslau.
Engraver. [Pazaurek]

Meyr Neffe, c. 1814-1900, Adolf im Böhmer-
wald, Bohemia.   Iridescent glass ware,
engraving, and decorating shop for Moorish
style vases.   Circa 1922, acquired by
Ludwig Moser's firm. [Arwas/Pazaurek]

Moriz Wenzel, Breslau, Bohemia. Retailer.
Managed by   Fran   Wenzel (d. 1921.)
[Pazaurek]

Minners Glass Co., N.Y., N.Y.   Trademark
active circa 1970s. [AGR]

Maryland Glass Corp.   Depression Glass,
early 20th century. [H.O.C.]

Majestic Cut Glass Co., Elmira, N.Y.,
1900/1918. [Farrar/Boggess]

Variety Glass Inc., Cambridge, Ohio.
Established in 1960.

    Sig.: Paperweights made by Tom Mosser.
[Melvin]

M

Chattanooga Glass Co., Baltimore, Md.
Trademark active circa 1970s. [AGR]

Klaus (b. 1936) and Isgard (b. 1941) Moje,
Hamburg. Modern designers.

Sig.: deeply cut

Kristalunie Maastricht, N. V., Glassworks
in Maastricht, Holland. Merged with De
Sphinx in 1925; in 1978, merged with
Leerdam. [van der Meer]

    Sig.: diamond point on base

Verrerie de la Paix, J. Mabut, Paris.
Glass retailer active circa 1900. [Hil-
schenz]

    Sig.: Engraved under foot of cameo vase.

Macbeth-Evans. Acquired by Corning Glass.
Trademarks for lamp chimneys. Heat resistant, tough and clear glass of high quality.

    Pearl Top: glass beads added for finish-
ing top rim. [Catalog]

MACBETH
No
PEARL GLASS

Denotes origin of a great many styles and qualities of glass made for export after World War I up to the present.

Sig.: usually acid stamped on base.

MADE IN CZECHOSLOVAKIA

Buffalo Cut Glass Co., Buffalo, N. Y. Circa 1902-18, cutting shop of Brilliant Period cut glass. [Daniels/Revi]

Marcel Duchamp (1887-1968), France. Avant-guard artist.

    Sig.: signed in diamond point on glass ampoule of Paris air. Issued in 1964 after a design produced in 1919. Number two of an edition of eight.

Marie Tesselschade (1594-1649), Nether-lands. Calligraphic diamond point designs. [Weiss]

Signed work known.

Marie. Not further identified. Possibly late 19th century. Attributed to France.

    Sig.: in gold on vase with flowers and tracery enamelled on light green glass. [Billiter]

Scott Depot Glass Co., Fort Smith, Ark. Trademark active circa 1970s, table & gift ware. [AGR]

Maurice Marinot (1882-1960), France. Circa 1911, began making Fauvre style colored glass. Retired circa 1937. [Arwas]

Sig.: acid etched or enameled, usually on side.

Mark Comfort Peiser, USA.   Studio artist, active circa 1970s.

MARK PEISER

Marmart Co., Ltd, London.   Retailers of glassware with painted decorations.   Trade name registered 1902. [Manely]

MARMART

Marquise de Sévigne, Paris Confectionery that used fancy packaging containers made by A. Walter about 1925.   France. [Klesse-Mayr]

Sig.: impressed under foot of covered bowl of pâte de verre.

also on same bowl impressed on side

and impressed on cover
Designed by Henri Bergé

A W N H B

Kings Co. Rich Cut Glass Works, Brooklyn, N.Y. Cutting shop of good quality work. Trade name active 1916. [Revi]

Master Glass Co., Clarksburg, W. Va. Trademark active circa 1970s. [AGR]

Mayflower Glass Works, Latrobe, Pa. Hand-made ware. Trademark active 1970s. [AGR]

Monica Bockstrom, Sweden. Designer at Boda c. 1970s. About 1964, used full signature. Before 1971, small works signed with initials. Circa 1971, began consecutive numbering. [Grover]

M B 4785 UNIK,
MONICA BOCKSTROM
w/ title & date

Mc D Bros. Not further identified. Believed to be American, early 20th century. [Boggess]

Sig.: acid stamped on brilliant cut glass bowl.

McKee Glass Co., established 1870. [Stout]

Sig.: molded on base after 1935 to 1940. Used on dinnerware and opaque kitchen ware.

McKanna Cut Glass Co., Honesdale, Pa. Cutting shop for brilliant cut glass, 1914–27. [Revi]

Trademark active circa 1915.

McKee & Brothers Glass Works, Pittsburgh, Pa. Established circa 1852, sold to Thatcher Glass Mfg. Co., in 1950. Made early flint glass, pressed milk glass, depression glass, etc. Makers of pressed glass, some of white opal in form of chickens. [Stout]

Sig.: molded on animals c. 1870s. Paper labels circa 1950s.

McKee

Molded on bread plate

Mc Kee

Burgun Schverer & Co., Meissenthal. [Traub/Klesse-Mayr]

Sig.: in black under foot, circa 1895–96.

Gillinder & Sons, Inc., Philadelphia, Pa., circa 1907.

Trademark for lighting wares: letters within a circular device.

MELILIYE

A. Goslett & Co., London. Maker of ornamental glass wares. Trademark registered 1884. [Manley]

Meriden Cut Glass Co., Meriden, Conn., 1895-1923. Cut glass for silver mountings by International Silver Co. [JCK]

Meunier. Not further identified.

    Sig.: in cameo on acid cut cameo vase

Drehobl Brothers Art Glass Co., Chicago, Ill. Established about 1919 by Frank J. Drehobl. Made stained glass windows for commercial and residential use and for juke boxes. [Darling]

M.G.

DREHOBL Bros

Marcel Goupy, France. C. 1909-1954, artistic director of Maison Georges Rouard. Wide range of objects, including table ware. [Arwas]

    Sig.: enamelled ware signed in enamels on base or side.

Maurice Heaton (b. 1900), Swiss origin, but of the American school of glass sculptors. Free lance worker. [Polak]

    Sig.: on decorated plaque.

M H 1971 / & title

M.H.

Hugo Max (1863-1896), Bohemia. Instructor at Steinschönau Trade School from 1898 to 1925. [Neuwirth]

Sig.: also with Fachschule initials.

M. H.

Michael Higgins, USA. (Born 1908, England) Studio artist; sculptures and plaques. [Grover]

MICHAEL HIGGINS 1972
also w/ title

Michigan Cut Glass Co., Lansing, Michigan, circa 1906-1911. Cutting shop for brilliant cut ware. [Revi/JCK]

MICHCUT

Attributed to Edward Michel, France, circa 1900. Scenic overlay cameo. [Blount] Edward Michel's works are artistically executed and rare. Generally, his works were either unsigned or signed "E Michel." [Blount/Arwas/BSMK]

Sig: cameo on cameo vase

≠ Michel
de Nancy

Charles Michel, Nancy, France. Industrial production cameo work with floral and scenic designs.

Sig.:

MICHEL NANCY

MICHEL PARIS

Gillinder & Sons, Philadelphia, Pa., circa 1900, label for lighting wares. [Peterson]

MICRA

Milla Weltmann, dates unknown. Designer for Loetz and Bakalowits, 19th century, Bohemia. [Arwas]

MiLLA WELTMANN LoETZ,

Edward Miller & Co., Meriden Conn., circa 1890s. Art lamps.

Sig: stamped in metal base.

MILLER

Applied Art Glass Co. Ltd., London, England. Trade name active circa 1975.

MIRRART PRODUCTS

Mission. Not identified. Molded on side of depression glass juice dispenser, circa 1920s or 30s. [Weatherman]

MISSION

Mitchell. Presumed American glass cutter in the brilliant style, early 20th century. [Boggess].

Sig.: diamond point

Mitchell

Unidentified designer at Steinschönau trade school, Bohemia. [Neuwirth]

M L 20

M. Model, France, c. 1930s. [Auction]

Sig.: impressed in mold blown figure of a bird.

M MODEL FRANCE

Moda.   Signed on products made at Daum Glass Works. [Bloch-Dermant/Blount]

Signed in cameo on acid cut cameo bowl with enamel decorations. [Blount]

MODA

Gill Brothers, Steubenville, Ohio, circa 1900. Lighting wares. [Peterson]

Trademark

Moe Bridges Co., Milwaukee, Wis. Active about 1910 to 1920. Maker of lamp bases and painted shades similar to those made by Handel.

Sig.: enameled on reverse painted shade. Metal base with molded "Moe Bridges Co./Milwaukee Wis.

MOE BRIDGES

Gottlob Samuel Mohn, (1789-1825). Worked with his father in Germany; in 1811, moved to Vienna. [Newman]

Signed on beaker with enameled land-scape, c. 1816. [Weiss]

MOHN FECIT 1816

Klaus (b. 1936) and Isgard (b. 1941) Moje. Glass designers in Hamburg making oven formed wares. In 1962, they established their own workshop; in 1967, made their first colored glass; in 1971, made their first heat formed glass. [Klesse-Mayr/MfK]

Sig.: diamond point on base
"HT" signifies high temperature firing.

MOJE
7974
HT/10
EXH

Clayton Mayer & Co. Ltd., London, England. Trade name active 1970s. Cut glass.

Gill Brothers Co., Steubenville, Ohio. Trademark registered 1897 for lighting wares. Etched or printed label. [Peterson]

Moncrieff's Glass Works, Perthshire, Scotland. John Moncrieff, c. 1922, began making decorative wares. "Monart" glass was developed in 1924, by Salvador Ysart (1887-1956). Made only by him and his son, Paul. The glass is clear, heavy, streaked with black, scarlet, and other Art Deco colors. Also maker of paperweights. Contemporary line of art glass called "Monax." [Arwas/Madley]

Trademark on paper label. One reference reports the original to be green, another reports the label as gold with black.

Molded in one inch diameter glass disc [Manely]

Monica Bockstrom, 20th century designer at Boda.

Sig.: engraved on base of ornamental wares.

Lockwood Bros., Sheffield, Eng. Glass manufacturers. Trademark registered 1888. [Manley]

MONARCH

Lion's head surrounded by "Monarch/Best Lead Flint" in outer band; "Oil Finished/-Fire Proof" inside band

MONCRIEFF SCOTLAND MONART

MB 4785 UNIK /
MONICA BOCKSTROM /
20/8 70 plus title

MONKEY

Manufactory Royale à Montcenis, France.
Sulphide lavelier plaque. [Cloak]

    Sig.: impressed on base

    and on sulphide of same plaque

MONTCENIS

ANDRIEU F

Montesy.   Probably France, 20th century.
Used on a cameo and intaglio decorated
vase. [Ptockv]

Legras et Cie, France. "Mont Joye" was a
line of cameo glass. [Hilschenz]

    Sig.: under foot in gilt on acid cut
    vase with gilt and enamel, usually on a
    transparent body. c. 1900.

Mosaic Shade Co. Inc., Chicago, Ill., circa
1909-29. [Darling]

    Sig.: stamped in metal edge of Tiffany-
    style shade, leaded with pastel and
    opalescent glass.

MOSAIC SHADE CO INC
CHICAGO

Verrerie Pochet et du Courval, Paris,
France. Perfume bottles, decor, novelties,
mosaics, pâte de verre. Trade name active
circa 1970s.

MOSAVER

Ludwig Moser & Söhne, Karlsbad, Bohemia.
Active from 1857 on. Established by Ludwig
Moser (1833-1916), glass engraver and mer-
chant. Established a manufactory at Meier-

höfen c. 1857.   In 1970, introduced limited
edition plates decorated with copper wheel
engravings. [Brohan/Kovel]

Sig.: circa 1940s, painted with white
enamel

Moser

Paper label

Engraved on side   (a) MOSER   (b) *Moser Karlsbad*

Added after World War I   *made in Cecho-Slovakia*

Etched on base of vase designed by Josef
Hoffmann, made by the Moser firm for the
Wiener Werkstätte, c. 1920. [Schweiger]

MOSER
CARLSBAD
W
CZECHO
SLOVAKIA

Moser Glassworks of Czechoslovakia at Karl-
ovy Vary (new names for Karlsbad and Ludwig
Moser firm).

Sig.: engraved on side

Lubos Metelak (b. 1934), at Moser since
1962, sculptor and engraver.

MOSER-1970-METELAK

Attributed to Koloman Moser (1868-1918), designer for the Wiener Werkstätte.

    Sig. [Auction]. Possibly misattributed. Koloman generally used a monogram.

Mountain Glass Co., Western, W. Va., USA. Table and gift ware, trademark active circa 1970s. [G & T]

Mount Washington. Paperweight of rainbow satin glass. Signature and authenticity questionable. [Auction]

MOUNT WASHINGTON

M. Petit, 18th c., Netherlands. Engraver in diamond point. [Weiss]

Signed work known.

Rudolph Müller, Bohemia. C. 1909/10, administrator and supervisor of glass house at Haida trade school. Date of association with Steinschönau unknown. [Neuwirth]

KK FS ST

Max Th. Rössler (b. 1893), Pachen. Trade school professor and engraver.

    Sig.: on early work

M R

    Later work.

Miluse Kytkova-Roubickova (b. 1922), Czechoslovakia. Sculptor. Designer for Council of Industrial Design.

M ROUBICKOVA 1971
also w/ title

M ROUBICKOVA-KYTKOVA
1967-72

Mount Vernon Glass Co., Mount Vernon, N. Y., circa 1810-36. Made bottles; also produced simple etched and cut designs on wares. [Daniels/McKearin]

Name of owner on a bottle seal under molded name of glass works.

Mt VERNON GLASS C^o

Mount Washington Glass Co., South Boston, Mass. Established 1837; resumed original name 1871. Circa 1894, acquired by Pairpoint. Mold blown and pressed art glass: "Burmese," "Royal Flemish," cut glass, etc.

Trademark: original is a paper label. Forgeries made of same form are acid etched. "Royal Flemish" ware gives an appearance of stained glass sections separated by raised gilt lines

Forgery made with black ink on Mt. Washington-type wares.

MT. W. G. CO.

Impressed in silver fittings of boxes, etc.

M. W.

Mulaty. Not further identified. Signature etched on an Art Deco item. [Auction]

MULATY

Muller Frères, established c. 1910 near Lunéville (Loraine), France, by Henri Muller and brother, Désiré, when joined with the glass works established c. 1900 by Henri Muller at Croismare. Art glass of many different types.

Sig.: cameo on 4 layer, 4 acid cut cameo
vase

MullerFreres
Luneville

Muller Fres
Lunéville

Engraved under foot of cameo vase

[signature: Crmuller Crimare fri Yang]

Other signature styles:

"Luneville" added after 1910
Engraved on side

MullerFres
Lunéville

MullerFres
Luneville

Signature on side,
shiny ground against
matt etching

Muller
(Roismare

Muller

Muller Fres
Luneville

Muller Fres
Luneville

Engraved on side
"Crosimare" added
after 1900;
signed in red
under foot

cameo

cameo

Welsbach Company, Gloucester City, N.J.
Trade name c. 1910 etched on lighting wares
[Peterson].

MULTI-FLEX

The Munich Studio, Chicago, c. 1903 to
1932. European style stained glass windows. [Darling]

Sig.: etched

The Munich Studio

Attributed to Toso, designer, Murano, Italy, circa 1950s. [Auction]

    Sig.: may include design number

MURANO /
ANTICA VETRERIA /
F 11: TOSO / 1854

Murmac Importing Corp, N.Y., N.Y. Distributors for foreign wares, trademark active c. 1970s.

Thomas Webb & Sons. Engraved by Ludwig Kny, circa 1890–1900. Vase made of "Murrhina" glass, internally decorated.

    Sig.: intaglio engraved

MURRHINA/TWC
(in monogram)/ LU KNY

Mount Washington Glass Co., USA. Circa 1870s stamped into metal fittings of decorated opal wares.

M. W.

Mills Walker & Co., Wordsley, England. Painted opal ware, late 1800s. [Manley]

M. W. & CO. VITRIFIED

Matthias Zwirn (b. 1623; active 1675), Switzerland. Painter of heraldic glass. [Gessert]

M·Z
1650

N

Anthonius Johannes van Kooten (1894-1951), Holland. Began working at Leerdam about 1930, made vases decorated with enamels and later produced lampwork. [Van der Meer]

"NS" in monogram. Not identified. Used on an Art Deco vase. [Auction]

NS

Niklaus Wirt, active 1583-1676, Switzerland. Painter of stained glass church windows. [Gessert]

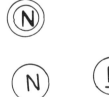

Northwood Glass Co., Martens Ferry, Ohio. C. 1880s to 1923. Maker of inexpensive pressed glass, utility and decorative items.

Sig.: used until 1910, molded in bottom of depression glass dish.

Other forms, usually in bottom of vessel:

Ober-Nester Glass Co., St. Louis, Mo., trademark for bottles and other utility items registered c. 1895 & 1948. Active c. 1970s, as division of Indian Head Inc.

North American Glass Co., Canada. C. 1883
to 1890. Containers and possibly brilliant
cut glass. [Stevens/Boggess]

Sig.: molded in bottom of containers.   N A G C

Acid etched on brilliant cut glass item

C. F. Monroe, Meriden, Conn. 19th century.
White opal ware decorated with pastel
colored enamels. [Revi]

Sig.: acid etched on box bottom.

Black ink signatures are to be regarded
with suspicion. [Cronin]

Nancea. Unidentified. [Auction/Blount]

Signed in enamel on a vase with three
layer acid cut cameo and enamel.

Mount Washington Glass Co., New Bedford,   NAPOLI
Mass. Trade name for clear glass with
internal and external decorations, c. 1900.
[Revi]

Nasan Oldo. Not further identified, circa   NASAN OLDO
1950s. Intaglio engraved design on vessel.
[Auction]

A. Douglas Nash (d. 1940). C. 1928, formed
the A. Douglas Nash Corp. when Tiffany

closed his glassworks.   Closed in 1931.
Nash developed "Chintz"   and "Silhouette"
glass. [Revi]

    Sig.: used after 1929. Seen on "Chintz"   NASH / 177 DD
    goblets

    Sig.: on gold iridescent vase.   NASH / QD 72

    Letters refer to color, numbers refer to
    size.

Henri Edouard Navarre (1885-1971), France.
C. 1924, started working with glass.
Molded glass bas-relief for luxury liner,
"Ile de France," c. 1927. [Arwas]

    Sig.: usually on base in diamond point.

    Used on a Cluthra-style vase   **NAVARRE 300**

    Crystal vase   NAVARRE 214

Nazeing Glass Works Ltd., England.   Trade   NAZEING
name active c. 1970s.   All types glasswares. [EGD]

Cambridge Glass Co., Cambridge, Ohio.
C. 1904, trade name for tablewares of
pressed patterns that resemble rich-cut
glass. [Revi]

    Sig.: molded in base.   NEARCUT

Gillinder & Sons, Philadelphia, Pa.   See: NEBULITE
Gillinder. Lighting wares [Peterson]

New England Glass Co., c. 1818-1890, East
Cambridge, Mass. Established by Deming
Jarvis and associates. Major maker of
glasswares, blown, flint, etc. Marks were
used on pressed wares, early flint glass.
[Fauster/McKearin]

Sig.: molded under base of lamp,
c. 1825-45. "E R" may refer to Enoch
Robinson, patenee.

N.E.G.CO./E.R. - S.R.

NEG/ER SR

Inscribed on brass fittings of lamp,
circa 1860.

N.E.G.CO.

Impressed on glass plug of silvered
double walled vessels, c. 1850-60.

NEGCO

May be cut or etched within a rectangle
any place on lamps, vessel handles or
sides, etc.

N.E. GLASS CO.

N E GL CO

Metal plate on lamp fittings, ca. 182545
to 1845

N. E. GLASS COMPANY /
BOSTON

Lacy salt dishes, c. 1825-50:
May have patent information in addition
to name

N & E /GLASS /COMPANY /
BOSTON

N. E. /GLASS /COMPANY/
BOSTON

N. E. GLASS CO.

Paper labels used on "Amberina," and
other types of art glass, c. 1880s.

N E G W/POMONA/
PAT'D/JUNE 15, 1886

N E G W/AGATA/
PAT'D/JAN 18, 1887

N E G W/WILD ROSE/
PAT'D/MAR 2, 1886

Newark Cut Glass Co., Newark, N.J.
C. 1906-1918, mail order distributor of
commercial quality brilliant cut glass.
[Revi]

    Trademark.

    Sig.: etched, about 12mm across shield

Kinrie T. Newcomb (b. 1945), USA. Studio
artist. Free-form vessels. [Grover]

NEWCOMB 1972

New England Glass Co. (1818-1890), East
Cambridge, Mass. See: N.E.G.Co.

    Signature cut or etched within a circle
    on base of vessels, c. 1865-75.

NEW ENGLAND GLASS CO.

    Old English style script used on a
    Centennial commemoration decanter set
    with wheel engraving, c. 1876.

NEW ENGLD /GLASS CO.
BOSTON

T. & W. Farmiloe, Middlesex, England. Glass
manufacturer.   Trademark   circa   1889.
[Manley]

Fostoria Glass Specialty Co., Fostoria, Ohio. Trade name for lighting wares c. early 1900s. [Peterson]

NOREC

Northwood Glass Co., Martins Ferry, Ohio. C. 1880s-1923. Inexpensive pressed dishes.

    Sig.: molded in bottom of vessel. Used on a carnival glass bowl.

Northwood

Jean Noverdy, Dijon, France. Exhibited c. 1926-28. Designer and operator of his own glass works producing industrial acid etched cameo. Also, operated a retail shop. [Arwas/Hilschenz]

    Sig.: acid etched with stencil against a mat ground.

Noverdy France

Nova Scotia Glass Co., New Glasgow, N.S. Containers, c. 1881-1892. [Stevens]

"N. S. G. CO." within a lozenge

Nyon, France. City where A. Duc de Caranza was located.

    Sig.: in red under foot [Bloch]

NYON 628

    also on same piece, signed on base:

A DE CARANZA

Imperial Glass Co., Trademark registered
c. 1921. [Revi]

Sig.: molded in pressed patterns of
rich-cut designs. Trademark registered
1911.

Molded in glass of iridescent ware.
Registered 1921

O

John S. O'Conner, 1890–1919, Hawley, Pa. Formerly a designer for C. Dorflinger. Opened his own cutting shop producing fine designs on good quality metal during the brilliant cut glass period. Trademark active. [Revi]

Arthur E. O'Conner, Goshen, N. Y. Son of John S. O'Conner of Hawley, Pa. Arthur operated the American Cut Glass Co., for his father, circa 1900–1902. They produced good quality wares. [Revi]

Oberhausener Glasfabrik, Funcke & Becker, Oberhausen, Germany. Drinkware. Trademark active circa 1970s. [Körting]

Ohio Cut Glass Co., N.Y, N.Y. Cutting shop established by Pitkin and Brooks, brilliant period. Burned in 1912. [Revi]

   Trademark:

Otto Pietsch, senior. Glass engraver at Steinschönau. [Pazaurek]

Otto Pietsch, junior.   Glass engraver at
Steinschönau. [Novy]

Johann Oertel Glass Factory, Haida, Czechoslovakia.   Established circa 1869. [Novy/
Bröhan]

    Trademark used since 1919:

    Sig.: etched   on   vase   with   Art   Deco
    designs.

    Engraved on foot

Oertel-Glas, Welzheim, Germany.   Trademark
active circa 1970s. Drinkware. [Körting]

Oiva Toikka (b. 1931), Finland.   Glass
sculptor and designer of other wares. In
1963, joined Notsjö Glass Works.

    Sig.: diamond point

OIVA TOIKKA/NUUTAJÄRVI
NOTSJÖ

Verrerie Louard S.A., Longray (Seine-
Maritime), France. Beauty products, pâte
de verre, mosaics for murals, and other.
Trade name active 1970s. [ANV]

OPALEX

James Augustus Jobling.   Trade name registered   circa   1920s;   later   acquired   by
Greener.

    Sig.: etched on base [Antique Coll. Cl.,
    Jan. '84.]

OPALIQUE / PATENT
APPLIED FOR

Orient and Flume, Chico, Calif. Established c. 1972. Paperweights, Art Nouveau revival lamp shades, iridescent glass, etc.

Sig.: engraved script, dated and numbered on base.   ORIENT AND FLUME

Orrefors Glasbruck, Sweden. Circa 1898, began making glass ink bottles and windows. After 1913, new ownership introduced broader lines. Now produces art glass, table ware, etc. Limited edition plates since 1970. Best pieces signed with full name of designer.

Sig.: engraved on base. May also have design number, designer, type of glass.   *Orrefors*

or Of

Denotes hand worked cut glass   A

Denotes machine fire polishing   U

Designed by Knut Bergqvist with Simon Gate, Advard Hald, and Heinrich Wollman, circa 1919.

ORREFORS/GRAAL/SG/KB/HW/no 481/19

Knut Bergqvist, c. 1919   "KB"

Gunnar Cyrén (b. 1931), at Orrefors since 1959.   ORREFORS EXPO B 548-67/ GUNNAR CYREN

Simon Gate (1883-1945), joined Orrefors in 1915. Instrumental in developing "Graal" glass.   G or SG

Orrefors Gate I s ts A-3.

Advard Hald (b. 1883), joined Orrefors in 1917. With Simon Gate developed cased glass.

ORREFORS H 314 1926 PL

1146C/EDWARD HALD/ORREFORS/ SWEDEN/GRAAL

ORREFORS/GRAAL NR 426P/ ADVARD HALD

Vicke Lindstrand (b. 1904). At Orrefors from 1928-41.

L

Orrefors Lindstrand 1841 AP. P

Ingegorg Lundin, to Orrefors in 1947.

D

ORREFORS/ ARIEL NR 567 H INGEGORG LUNDIN

ORREFORS/ ARIEL DU 546/INGEORG LUNDIN

Nils Landberg (b. 1907). In 1925, came to Orrefors

N

ORREFORS/LANDBERG 30088 B6 BS

Edvin Ohrström (b. 1906), to Orrefors circa 1936, developed "Ariel" glass.

F

ORREFORS/1956/E OHRSTROM

ORREFORS SWEDEN/ARIEL NO 284/ E OHRSTROM

Diamond point: F. Hald and K. Bergqvist, circa 1917, Graal glass

SG-KB

Sven Palmqvist (b. 1921). At Orrefors since 1936, developed "Karak" and "Ravenna" glass.

P

ORREFORS PALMQVIST 1877 AK SR

ORREFORS/KARAK NR 436/ SVEN PALMQVIST

Orrefors P2765 2u

John Selbing (b. 1908), at Orrefors since 1927.

C

Jan Johansson. Designer. Internally decorated vessel circa 1970s.

ORREFORS EXPO J 354-74 / JAN JOHANSSON

Orivit, Oberzwieselau. Circa 1906, art metal and crystal factory. Designs by Georg Carl von Reichenbach. [Schrack]

Sig.: on metal mounts of a goblet and a vase

"Orivit"

F. & C. Osler, Birmingham, Eng. Established 1807, cut glass, chandeliers, epergnes. Also, molded busts, painted and opalescent wares.

OSLER

Ovington Brothers, N.Y.,N.Y. Exclusive retail shop for tableware, art glass, etc. Trade name registered circa 1895, circa 1942, trade name renewed. [Peterson]

Sig.: label or acid etched, often includes name of designer or maker

OVINGTON

P

Heinrich Pietsch (b. 1873), from a large family of glass cutters and designers in Steinschönau, Bohemia. Operated a glass works. [Pazaurek]

Philipp Hahn (b. 1815), in Paris until World War I, then moved to Geneva, Switz. Engraver. Also see: Philipp Hanh. [Pazaurek]

Honesdale Cut Glass under ownership of Carl Frances Prosch (1864-1937). See: Honesdale. Cut glass. Used about 1916.

Pairpoint Glass Works, New Bedford, Massachusetts. Established 1865. In 1894, acquired Mt. Washington Glass Works. [Padgett]

Sig.: may be scratched on items by special request.

Etched on cut glass

Paperweights with white "P" in a blue arch or a yellow free floating "P."

May also be engraved with number and year.

"Rose" weights are dated by color of
rose:
1972 red
1973 yellow
1974 amethyst

Snake weights dated by color of snake:-
1972 amethyst
1973 opal with green or blue snake
1974 French blue with blue or green
snake

Verrerie Parant, S.A., Trelon, France.
Trademark active c. 1970s.

P

F. X. Parsche & Son Co., Chicago, Ill.
1902-25. Cutting shop brilliant period cut
glass. Fine pieces designed and cut for
special orders. [JCK/Revi]

Pennsylvania Glass Products Co., Pittsburgh, Pa. Trademark active c. 1970s.
[AGR]

Pierce Glass, Indian Head, Inc., Port
Allegany, Pa. Trademark active c. 1970s.
[AGR]

Perthshire, Crieff, Scotland. Established
1961. Paperweights in special limited editions, yearly limited editions, and un-

limited editions. [Selman]

    Sig.: date and signature cane or diamond
point on base

    Since 1969 yearly limited editions with
date letter imbedded in top design:
      1969   A
      1970   B
      1971,   C
      etc. until 1980   L

    Selected items with artists initials on
base in diamond point:
Jack Allen, Master Blower   J A

    Anton Moravec, faceting   A M

Otis A. Mygatt, N.Y., N.Y. Lighting wares   PAGODA
c. 1900. [Peterson]

Pairpoint Glass Co., New Bedford, Mass.,
c. 1865-96. Pairpoint Corp., 1896 to 1938.
Acquired Mt. Washington Glass Works in
1894.   In   1952,   became   Gundersen-
Pairpoint. Closed in 1958. [Auila/
Padgett]

    Sig.: decorated opal-ware box.   PAIRPOINT MANUFACTURING
                                                  COMPANY/4634/57

    Paper label c. 1970-72

1972 on

Modern items made in Spain for Pair-point.

Gundersen-Pairpoint, paper label

Limited edition plates started in 1972-73.

Metal lamp bases always stamped. Art shades often stamped on lower shade rim:

THE PAIRPOINT CORP'N

Blown-out and scenic shades occasionally include:

PATENTED JULY 9, 1907

Pairpoint Corp

H K

Artists' signatures, signed in diamond point or painted, may be found on shades. [Padgett]

Palme. Lampshade painter for Handel Co. Early 20th century. [Grant]

PAL

Austin D. Palmer, Coshocton, Ohio. Trademark registered 1892. Souvenir objects for World's Fair. [Peterson]

Les Fères Pannier, Escalier de Cristal.
Established before 1874, France. Retailer
of fine wares. Alphonse Reyen, designer
[Bloch]

Sig.: diamond point

PANNIER FRÈRES

PANNIER - ESCALIER DE CRISTAL

Cristallerie de Pantin, France. C. 1910
[Arwas]

Sig.: gilt

John Davenport, England. Decorative process
to imitate etchings, patented 1806. Surface
coated with thin layer powered glass paste,
design scratched in. When fused to body,
gave effect like acid engraving. [Revi]

PATENT

Used on Mother-of-Pearl glass. Origin
doubtful.

PATENT

United States Patent Office, Washington,
D.C. By knowing patent date, one can refer
to United States Patent Office records to
determine assignee.

Patented Mar. 1887

Year patent issued	Patent number
1836–1840	1 – 1,922
1841–1850	1,923 – 7,864
1851–1860	7,865 – 31,004
1861–1870	31,005 – 110,616
1871–1880	110,617 – 236,136
1881–1890	236,137 – 443,986
1891–1900	443,987 – 664,826
1901–1920	664,827 – 1,326,898
1921–1930	1,326,899 – 1,787,423

Pauline Solven (b. 1943), England. Sculptures. Helped establish "The Glasshouse," Covent Garden, London.

PAULINE SOLVEN 1971

Paul Wissmach Glass Co., Paden City, W. Va. Trademark active 1970s. [AGR]

Paulus Eder, Nuremberg, Germany. Active 1685–1709. Tiefschnitt engraving with great detail. [Weiss]

PAULUS EDER FECIT.

Pietro Bigaglia, Murano, Italy. Millefiori paperweight with date: "1845." Earliest maker of millefiori weights.

Siganture and date cane

P B

Pitkin & Brooks, Chicago, Ill. Active 1872 to 1915. Maker of blanks and cutting shop for Brilliant Period cut glass.

Trademark:

Sig.: etched

Probably forgery [Cronin]:

P & B CO

Paul D'Avesn, France.   Active 1920s-30s.
Frosted ware influenced by Lalique. Some
ware washed with opaque paint contrasting
with glass surface. Signed all work.

Sig.: etched on underside of base

P. Eiselt, Steinschönau, Bohemia.   Glass
engraver early 1900s. [Pazaurek/Benezit]

Mount Washington Glass Co. "Peach Blow," a
patented art glass that shades from pale
blue to pink, patented 1885 by Frederick
Shirley, worker at Mount Washington. The
"Peach Skin" was an acid finish to give the
soft look of peach fuzz.

Paper label

Peach skin
like finish

Macbeth-Evans Glass Co., Pittsburgh, Pa.
Pearl top decorated lamp chimneys, patented
circa 1883, for chimneys decorated with
applied glass beads about top rim.

Sig.: etched

Pears & Co., Pittsburgh, Pa. [Auction]

    Sig.; molded in flint glass pressed salt
    dips

PEARS

Peerless Cut Glass Co., Deposit, N.Y.
Established 1905 to about 1913, operated by
Kelly & Steinman. [Revi]

PEERLESS

Standard Oil Co., N.Y., N.Y. Used on lamp
accessories early 20th century. [Peterson]

"PEERLESS AMERICAN"
with Indian's head in
profile facing left

Peill & Putzler Glashüttenwerke, Düren,
Germany. Active 1970s, producers of drink-
wares. [Körting]

Pellatt & Green, England. Aspley Pellatt
(1791-1863), in 1819 patented cristallo-
cameo technique of imbedding cameo work
into glass casing. [Wakefield]

    Sig.: molded under cameo profile on both

PELLATT & GREEN PATENTEES/
LONDON

PELLATT & CO. PATENTEES

Penrose Glasshouse, Waterford, Ireland.
1783-1851. [Davis]

    Sig.: molded in decanter base in circu-
    lar format

PENROSE, WATERFORD

Harris & Sheldon, Ltd., Birmingham, England.   Trade   name   registered   1903. [Manley]

PERMENART

Perthius, Paris, France. C. 1900.

    Sig.: enameled on base of cameo and enamel decorated vase.

PERTHUIS PARIS

Jean Perzel, designer c. 1935, France. [Auction]

    Signed on pair of brass and frosted glass sconces.

PERZEL

Peter Wolff, Cologne, Ger.   Active 1660-1677. Engraver using diamond point and incised motifs on römers. Works show Dutch influence in the Coats of Arms and landscapes. [Newman]

PETER WOLFF

George H. Holgate, Philadelphia, Pa. Circa 1905. Lamps. [Peterson]

PETROLITE

Not identified. Used on opaque white glass with enamel Chinoiserie decoration. Probably 18th century English, area of Newcastle. [Newman]

"PF" or "PP"

Portland Glass Co., Portland, Maine. 1863-1873. Pressed glass. [Davis]

    Sig.: molded on a swan

P G CO PATENT

N. O. Phelps & Son, Rochester, N. Y. Trademark active c. 1970s. Hand-cut crystal. [AGR]

Philip Boileau, 19th c., U.S.A. Signed picture of "Gibson Girl" on lid of box marked: "Wave Crest." See: Mount Washington Glass Co. [Auction]

PHILIP BOILEAU
COPYRIGHT 1907

Philipp Hahn (b. 1814). In Paris until World War I, then moved to Geneva, Switz. Engraver.

    Sig.: engraved on a plaque

PHILIPP HAHN

Pavel Hlava (b. 1924), Czech. Designer of free form, cut glass, utility stemware, etc.

    Designed for Moser Glassworks

P. HLAVA/
CZECHOSLOVAKIA

P. HLAVA 1966

PAVEL HLAVA, MOSER

Phoenix Glass Co., Pittsburgh, Pa. Established 1880. Maker of lampshades, bottles, lamps, sculptured decorative ware, etc.

    Trademark registered 1881

    Trademark registered 1896. Etched on lighting accessories

PHOENIX VOLLENDEN WARE

Verrerie et Ateliers Waltersperger, Blangy-sur-Bresle, France. Perfume atomizers, lamp bases, hand-made art glass. Trade name active 1906. [NAV]

PIALA

Glasmanufaktur Friedrich Pietsch, Stein-schönau, North Bohemia. Late 19th or early 20th century.

    Sig.: Cameo box with cameo sig.

Pilgrim Glass Co., Ceredo, W. Va. Trade-mark active 1970s. Paperweights designed by Robert Moretti and other decorative items. [AGR/Melvin]

Pilkington Brothers, British. Established 1826. Flat and other industrial glass.

Pirelli Glass, England. Glass figures and decorative items. Trade name active 1970s. [EGD]

PIRELLI GLASS

Stourbridge Flint Glass Works, Pittsburgh, Pa. Established by J. Robinson & Son, c. 1830. [Innes]

    Sig.: molded in lacy salt

PITTSBURGH

Pieter Kibon (1737-1826), Haarlem. En-graver in diamond point, used English glasses. [Weiss]

P. K.

Philip Kiluk, U. S. A..   Painter at
Pairpoint, 20th century.

    Sig.: early

PK ⟨p⟩

10/14/70

    Later style, used on vase

P. KiLUK ⟨P⟩699

Pete Lewis, Millville, N.J.   Miniatures.
[Selman]

    Sig.: limited edition paperweight cane
    c. 1978. Some with date cane.

⟨PL⟩ ⟨1973⟩

Verrerie Pochet et du Courval, Paris.
Perfume bottles, commercial mosaics and
pâte de verre.   Trade name active 1906.
[ANV]

PLASTEMERI

Pittsburg Lamp, Brass and Glass Co. Pittsburgh, Pa. C. 1920s. [Auction]

    Sig.: label on reverse painted lamp
    shade.

P. L. B. & G. CO.

A. H. Heisey & Co., Newark, Ohio.   Trade
name registered c. 1905 for pressed domestic wares, pressed. [Peterson]

PLUNGER CUT

P. Luyten, Netherlands.   Probably 17th
century. Works known in diamond point and
stipple. [Weiss]

Exact signature form
not known

Pavel Molnàr (b. 1940), Munich, Germany.
Maker of modern vessels. [Klesse]

    Sig.: diamond point under base, circa
1960s

P. Nicolas (1875-1952), Nancy, France.
Worked at Emile Galle's after his military
service until 1914. In 1919, opened his
own studio. Also designed for the St.
Louis les Bitches. Collaborated with
Mercier. From 1919 to 1925, signed his
work "d'Argental" (meaning Valley of Silver, a region near St. Louis). From 1925
to 1928, he used both signatures; after
1928, he used only "P. Nicolas." [Bloch-
Dermant]

    Sig.: engraved on cameo vase

P. Nicolas
et Mercier
St Louis
Nancy

Gleason-Tiebout Glass Co., N.Y., N.Y. Used
on lighting ware. [Peterson]

POLYCASE

Porte & Markle. Retailers of brilliant
style cut glass by Roden.

PORTE & MARKLE

Verrerie Réunis de Vallérysthal et Portieux, Paris. Trade name active c. 1970s.
Decorative table ware and art glass.

PORTIEUX VALLERYSTHAL

Portieux Verriende, Portieux, France,
active 1860-70. [ANV]

    Sig.: Used on enamel decorated cordial
glass.

PORTIEUX VERRIENDE

Bruno Posselt GmbH., Germany. Hand cut
lead crystal. Trade name active 1970s.

POSSELT

PP or PR unidentified 18th century decorator who used enamels on opaque white
glass. [Charleston]

McKee-Jeannette Glass Works, Jeannette, Pa.
Molded in pressed cut wares that copy
brilliant-cut glass design. Used from 1904
to 1930s. Trademark registered 1913.

Sig.: molded

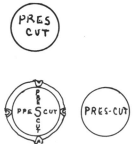

Price's Patent Candle Co., London. Trademark patented 1884 for lighting device.
[Manley/Peterson]

Professor Josef Hoffmann (1870-1936), Austria. Founding member of Wiener Sezession
and Wiener Werkstätte. Designer for Loetz
Witwe.

Sig.: engraved with wheel, c. 1913

PrOF, HOFFMANN

Professor Konrad Habermeier (b. 1907),
Germany. Assistant at Stuttgart trade
school under W. von Eiff. Head of glass
department at Schwäbisch Gmünd trade
school.

PROF. K. HABERMEIER
GRALGLAS

Professor Michael Powolny (1871-1954), Austria.   Designer for Lobmeyr and Loetz.
Member of Vienna Secession.   From 1891 to
1894, at Industrial Arts School, Stiermark,
Austria. [Pazaurek]

    Sig.: wheel engraved

Prof. Powolny
Loetz

Paul Joseph Stankard (b. 1942), Mantua,
N.J. Paperweights in editions of 25 to 75
pieces. Botanical designs after the Blaschka   Collection,   Harvard   University.
[Selman]

    Sig: signature cane; incised edition
    number, date, & copyright symbol

    Early pieces etched on base or on side,
    or placed in a cane

    After 1981, signature cane at base of
    colored   weights or on side of clear
    ones.

P. Schelling, Holland.   Designer at Leerdam
since 1933.

    Sig.: diamond point script

P. SCHELLING

Paul Ysart Ltd., Scotland.   Established
about 1972 by Paul Ysart (b. 1904). Paperweights. [Selman]

    Sig.: in cane

Paper label

Clarke's Fairy Light, 19th century England.

    Trade name   PYRAMID

    Trademark

Corning Glass Co., Corning, N.Y. Heat resistant glass developed in 1912 to use for railway lantern glass which broke during rains.

P. Zwart, Holland. Worked at Maastricht circa 1928-29. [Van der Meer]

Q

Quaker City Cut Glass Co., Philadelphia, Pa.   Active 1902 to about 1924.   Cutting shop for Brilliant Period cut glass. Trademark used on paper label. [Revi]

J. Mortlock & Co., London.   Retailer of glass wares made by Sowerby, circa 1870's.

QUEEN ANN CANDLESTICK

    Sig.: candlesticks of opaque pressed glass in neo-classical style.   Words molded on raised disk on base. [Manley]

Quezal Art Glass and Decorating Co., N.Y., N.Y.   C. 1901-25, art glass of several types.   Established by Martin Bach & Thomas Johnson, workers from Tiffany. [Roberts]

    Sig.: wheel engraved, horizontal straight lines that are dished out, letters 1/16" to $\frac{1}{4}$" high.

Quezal

    Letters are gilt in finest work, black or silver on standard work.

    Small shades signed on side closest to viewer;   "Lily" lights, on outside of shade on collet.

    C. 1920's, acid etched

    Fake signatures etched with electric tool, letters have square sides and flat bottoms.

R

Mount Washington Glass Co. C. 1837–1869
located at South Boston, from 1869–1896 at
New Bedford, Mass. Tablewares and art
glass. Trademark registered 1892. [Revi]

    Sig.: trademark printed in red on
"Royal Flemish" wares.

R. G. (?) Not identified, possibly French
c. 1900.

    Sig.: relief etched on side of vase of
clear color with multiple colored overlay with etching.

Richard Horn, 20th century. Art Deco style
designs. [Novy Bor]

    Sig.: wheel engraved

Richard Süssmuth (b. 1900). Worked at
Dresden Trade School.

See: Riedel. Austria , circa 1980s.
[Merchandise Mart]

    Sig.: c. 1980s, stencil etched on
engraved plate

Arthur Klose, Breslau. Engraver.

Wilem Jacob Rozendaal (b. 1899), Holland. Designer from 1924-28 at De Sphink; 1928 to 1929 (or 1933) at Maastricht.[Van der Meer]

    Sig.: Used while at Maastricht

    Other signature style; date not con-firmed:

William Runge, lamp shade painter at Handel Company. Early 20th century. [Grant]

R

C. F. Rumpp & Sons, Inc. Philadelphia, Pa. Trademark registered 1892, tablewares.

Roden Brothers, Ltd., Toronto, Ontario, Canada. Brilliant Period glass cuttimg shop, mostly with floral designs. Trade-mark active 1915. [Boggess]

    Sig.: acid etched

Viking Glass Co., Rainbow Art Glass Divi-sion. Active 1970s.

    Paper labels.

McKee Glass Co.   C. 1940s & 50s.   Heat
resistant kitchen-ware. [Stout]

    Sig.: molded in glass   RANGE – TEC

Raoul Goldoni (b. 1919), Yugoslavia. Began
working with glass in 1958 as design con-
sultant in Yugoslavia and Italy. Sculptured forms.

    Sig.: engraved. Date and title may be   RAOUL GOLDONI
    added.

R. B. Curling & Sons, Fort Pitt, Pa., circa
1829-1832, pressed table and decorative
wares. [Innes]

    Sig.: molded   R. B. CURLING & SONS/
                                          FORT PITT

British Registry Mark for designs, used
from 1842 to 1883. Glass is Class III.
Printed on or molded in ware.

1842-1867 year letter at top of diamond

A	1854	N	1864
B	1858	O	1862
C	1844	P	1851
D	1852	Q	1866
E	1855	R	1861
F	1847	S	1849
G	1863	T	1867
H	1843	U	1848
I	1846	V	1850
J	1854	W	1865
K	1857	X	1842
L	1856	Y	1853
M	1859	Z	1860

1868-1883 year letter on diamond's
right:

A	1871	L	1882
C	1878	P	1877
D	1879	S	1875
E	1881	U	1874
F	1873	V	1876
H	1869	W	Mar 1 to 6 1878
I	1872		
J	1880	X	1868
K	1883	Y	1879

Month Letter Both Periods

A   December
B   October
C or O   January

D   September
E   May
G   February

(K   December in 1860)
M   June
R   August

(R   Sept. 1-19, 1857)
W   March

Welsbach Company, Gloucester City, N.J.
Lamp chimneys, acid etched stamp, trade
name registered about 1908. [Peterson]

REFLEXOLIER

British Registry number for designs.
Number beginning in January:

Reg. 16,898
or other number

1	1884
141,273	1890
246,975	1895
351,202	1900
447,000	1905

Lippincott Glass Co., Cincinnati, O. Trade
name for lighting wares, registered about
1896. [Peterson]

REGAL

Royal Glass Co., Centralia, Ill. Trademark
registered in 1910.   Windows, enameled
wares, etc. [Peterson]

Reha Glass Co., Chicago, Ill. Table and
gift ware.   Trademark active 1970s.
[G & T]

Reijmyre Glassworks, Ostergötland, Sweden.
C. 1810-1826, resumed operation in 1936 for
table and contemporary art wares. Circa
1890s, produced Gallé inspired cameo work.
[Neuwirth]

    Sig.: C. 1905, gilt engraved on side of
    vessel.

    On same piece, on underside:
    May also include designer's name or
    "Unica."

Reijmyre
Suède

_No. 117_

Rexxford, Bavaria, Germany. Limited edition bowls circa 1974. [Kovel]

Believed to be signed

See: Raoul Goldoni, Yugoslavia. Sculptor.
[MfK]

R Goldoni

R. Henry, Cambridge, Ohio. [Etling]

    Sig.: moulded

Richard. Lorraine, France. Mostly two-
layer commercial grade cameo with florals
and landscapes, c. 1920s. [Hilschenz]

    Sig.: cameo

Richard

Richard

Henry G. Richardson & Sons, Wordsley, England. Sold to Thomas Webb about 1930. Glass manufacturer.

Trademark registration date not known

Trade name active c. 1970s for table glass

RICHARDSON

W. H. B., & B. & J. Richardson, Wordsley, Eng. C. 1836 to about 1850 when it became Henry G. Richardson & Sons. [Manley/ Wakefield]

Sig: enamel decoration and signature. Early decorations were black; later, polychrome. One piece of each set was signed.

RICHARDSON'S VITRIFIED

RICHARDSON'S VIRTIFIED ENAMEL COLOURS

Signed on vessel with classical figures painted in iron red

RICHARDSON'S STOURBRIDGE

Riedel Glass Works, Austria. Established 1750.

Trademark active 1970s.

Nancy Still (b. 1926), designer at Riihi-mäen Lasi Oy Glass Works, Riihimäki, Finland. Since 1928, the factory has included art glass in production lines.

Sig.: Sculpture c. 1970s
May include title

RIIHIMÄEN LASI OY FINLAND,
NANCY STILL.

Daniel C. Ripley established Ripley & Co., after 1874 when he left partnership with George Duncan. [Innes]

Sig.: on a lamp

RIPLEY & CO.
PATND PENDING

Roland Jahn (b. 1934 in Germany). Working
in U.S.A. leading workshops and teaching.

    Sig.: on free-from vase

R. JAHN 1971

Rufin Koppel (b. 1898), Altheide. Engraver
of classical subjects. [Pazaurek]

RK

S. Reich & Co., Krasna, Bohemia. Large
producers of early industrial acid etched
cameo. C. 1900.

RKrasna

René Jules Lalique (1860–1945), founder of
Cristallerie Lalique et Cie, France. Circa
1908, established glass factory to produce
molded, pressed, and engraved decorative
wares, many with surface treatment of acid
etching or sandblasting to produce frosted
appearance. In 1965, began to make limited
edition plates, in 1976, limited edition
sculptures.

    Sig.: earliest style, engraved on rim of
base with model number. "France" used
for export wares.

R. Lalique
France N⁰ - - -

During the later 1920, model numbers
discontinued, name molded in low relief
or acid etched with stencil.

Engraved

R LALIQUE
FRANCE

Molded

R LALIQUE

R LALIQUE

R. LALIQUE

Molded on blown wares

R. LALIQUE

Diamond point, attributed to Lalique

R Lalique
France

Diamond point, c. 1924

R Lalique

Used on perfume bottle. Lack of definition suggests that initials were stamped onto blown vessel while still soft.

Sandblasted over stencil

R. LALIQUE
FRANCE

Inscribed

R. LALIQUE

and molded on same plate. Verrerie
d'Alsace, opened in 1921. Operated for
a brief period, presumed only for
production of tableware

Vd'A / FRANCE

Many items of frosted glass bear Lalique
marks. Beware of items with mold seams,
acid etched marks with ghost image, and
those marked "Made in France." See
"Lalique" for additional forms

R. Moretti (b. 1930), Murano, Italy.
Paperweight maker at Pilgrim Glass Corp.,
USA. [Melvin]

R. MORETTI

Robert E. Naess (b. 1943), Calif. Teacher
and studio artist. [Grover]

R. NAESS '69

Launay — Hautin et Cie, France. In 1843,
Jean-François Robert began a glass decorating studio at Sèvres Porcelain Works,
produced work of good quality. [Amic]

   Sig.: printed in red on back of opaline
vases.

Le Verre Français, France. Established in 1913 by Ernest and Charles Schneider (1881-1962). Produced art glass. [Arwas/ Schack]

Sig.: acid etched on pieces after designs by Robert Schneider, 1955-60.

Robert SCHNEIDER Edna par Schneider France

Robert Wilson, U.S.A. Individual sculptures. Designer for Barbini, Murano, Italy. Graduated from Univ. of Texas in 1934. [Grover]

Sig.: may appear with title

ROBERT WILSON

Robj, Paris. Retailer c. 1920s-1930s. Commissioned artists to design his lines. Some work may include name of designer. [Uecker]

Sig.: molded on side of panel of table lamp.

Robj PARIS

Verreries Domec, Bordeaux, France. Decorative and industrial wares. Trade name active c. 1970s.

ROCDUR

Rochette, U.S.A. Lamp shade painter for Handel Company, early 20th century. [Grant]

Sig.: used on cased glass shade, with Art Nouveau design in a cameo technique.

ROCHETTE

Rocknow (?). Lamp shade painter for Handel
Co., circa 1900. [Auction]

  Signed on a Teroma shade with Handel's
  mark and #4222.

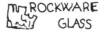ROCKNOW (?)

W. A. Bailey & Co., London. Glass manufacturer. Trademark registered about 1908.
[Manley]

ROCKWARE GLASS

Roger. Not identified.

  Signed in cameo on a cameo vase.
  [Blount]

Roger

United States Glass Co., Pittsburgh, Pa.
Trademark registered c. 1911. Label on
domestic wares.

Elias Rosbach (1670-1765). Senior master
of Berlin glass engravers' guild.
[Newman/Weiss]

  Sig.: engraved in diamond point script
  on foot of intaglio engraved goblet.

ROSBACH GESCH: / BERLIN

Rosbach Fecit Berlin

Per Lütken (b. 1916), Denmark. In 1924 came to Holmegaard Glass Works; since 1970s, chief designer.

PER LUTKEN,
HOLMEGAARD 2382/ R 1970

Mount Washington Glass Co., New Bedford, Mass. Trade name for art glass copied after Libbey's "Amberina." Name registered 1884.

ROSE AMBER

Rosenthal, Selb, Germany. Limited edition glass sculptures, introduced in 1974. [Kovel]

Exact signature form not known

Rene Roubicek (b. 1922), Prague, Czech. Since 1945, designer at Novy Bor. Sculptures.

ROUBICEK

Roux Chalon. Not identified. [Grover]

Signed on cameo ewer.

ROUX CHALON A R
SOANE

E. E. Rowley, cameo artist at Stevens & Williams, England.

Exact signature form not known

Franz A. Mehlem, Bonn, Germany. Established in 1775. Trademark registered 1890. Maker of porcelain tablewares. [Honey/ Peterson]
Doubtful if used as permanent mark for glasswares.

H. Perilstein, Philadelphia, Pa. Trademark registered c. 1906 for cut and other decorative ware. [Peterson]

Royal Castle, England. Trademark active 1970s for table and gift wares. [G & T]

Royal Germania. Limited edition paperweights and plates introduced in 1970, goblets in 1972. [Kovel]

Believed to be signed

Leerdam Glass Works, Netherlands. Trademark active c. 1970s for decorative wares.

Royal Netherlands Glass Works, Holland. Established 1834 . Limited edition plates since 1973. [Kovel/G & T]

St. Louis Glassworks, France. [Selman]

    Sig.: on base of sulphide commemorative paperweight

Mount Washington Glass Co. In 1894, bought
by Pairpoint Corp. Trademarks for cut
glass: c. 1837-1869 at South Boston,
1869-1896 at New Bedford.
[Newman/Peterson]

   Trademark   registered   c. 1882   by
   Frederick S. Shirley, glass worker

Ruth Maria Kilby, born in Czech. Worked in
U.S.A.   In 1948, began experiments in
translucent effect of glass for murals and
plaques.

   Sig.: may also include title   RUTH KILBY 1962

S

Sroeke (?). Not further identified. Etched on brilliant cut glass. [Boggess]

Josef Emil Schneckendorf (1865–1945), Germany. Designer of art glass, such as mother-of-pearl, iridescent, etc. Simple shapes with floral or swirl designs. Circa 1907, was director of Edel Glass Workshop for the Grand Duke Ernst Ludwig Heissen. Designed in the Jugendstil. [Arwas/ Neuwirth]

    Sig.: iridescent script on bottom, c. 1908

    Designed for the Grand Duke with crown and E L monogram.

Not identified. Possibly North Bohemia, c. 1900. Used on iridescent and enameled vase.

Albin Schaedel, Germany. Active 1970s. Designer. [M.F.K.]

H. P. Sinclair & Co. (1904-28), Corning,
N.Y.   Fine   engraved   and   cut   wares.
[Farrar]

    Sig.: acid etched.

    Forgeries of various sizes and qualities
    exist.

Steuben Glass Co.   Used for a short time
after 1932. [Gardner]

S

    Sig.: diamond point

Paul Stankard.   Paperweight designer at
Moncrieff Glassworks, Perth, Scotland from
1948 on. [Selman]

    Signature cane with edition and number
    in diamond point on bottom

Strathearn Ltd., Scotland.   Circa 1967.
Acquired Vasart. [Cloak]

    Sig.: in cane of paperweight   S

Richard Süssmuth Glashütte, Immenhausen,
Germany.   Drinkware.   Trademark active
c. 1970s. [Körting/G & T]

Maurius-Ernest Sabino (b. 1871), Paris.
C. 1920s director of glass works. Closed
during World War II, reopened c. 1960s.
Lamps, vases, figures etc. After 1960,
made mainly small birds and nudes. Circa
1970s, limited edition plates. Export ware
marked with "France." [Arwas]

Sig.: engraved on bottom

Sabino Sabino
Paris France

Molded

SABINO FRANCE

SABINO PARIS

Jean Sala (b. 1895), Paris. Made extensive
use of bubbled glass in design. [Arwas]

Sala

Salviati & Co., Murano, Italy. Established
1856 by Antonio Salviati. Fine art and
other wares. [Arwas/Newman]

Sig.:

Luciano Gaspari, C. 1970s designer.
Signed in diamond point.

SALVIATI & CO.

SALVIATI S G DESIGNED
BY L. GASPARI /
FOR SALVIATI

Giorgio Taventi. Diamond point.

SALVIATI & CO. /
DESIGNED BY GIORGIO
TAVENTI FOR SALVIATI

T. H. Salviati, designer.

DESIGN BY TH. SALVIATI
DESIGN STUDIO

Salzburger Cristallglas-Gesellschaft, Salz-
burg, Austria.   Drinkware.   Trademark
active c. 1970s. [Körting/G & T]

Gill Brothers Co., Steubenville, Ohio.
Trademark registered c. 1887.   Label or
etched on chimneys. [Peterson]

SAMSON

Samuel J. Herman (b. 1936). Worked in USA
and London.   Designed line for Val St.
Lambert. Maker of studio glass. [MFK]

   Sig.: engraved on base of sculptural
vase.

Samuel J Herma
1973

Samues Schwartz (1681-1737), Thuringia/
Arnstadt.   C. 1713, court engraver at
Gotha. [Weiss]

SAMUES SCHWARTZ FECT.
ANNO 1712

Boston & Sandwich Glass Co., Mass. Pressed
glass, useful items. [McKearin]

   Sig.: molded in base of salt dish

SANDWICH

Sanel, France.   Not further identified,
possibly 1940s. [Auction]

   Sig.: used on acid cut cameo vase,
signed in cameo.

SANEL

   Molded on same vase:

MADE IN FRANCE

Andreas Friedrich Sang (active 1719-60), Weiman. [Weiss] See: A. F. Sang.

SANG

Paolo Santini (b. 1929), Florence, Italy. Designed for Daum of France.

SANTINI/1968-150/DAUM
and title.

Pierre Honoré Boudon de Saint-Amans (1774-1858), Paris. In 1818, obtained patent for making cameos enclosed in glass. [Weiss]

    Sig.: on sulphide portrait

S. A. PARIS

Legras, St. Denis. Reverse spelling of "Legras." Used on cameo work that simulates hardstone carving with enamel enhancements. [Blount]

    Sig.: cameo script

SARGEL SD

Sarlandie, Limoges, France. C. 1925. Used on enameled vase. [Auction]

SARLANDIE/LIMOGES

Société Autonome de Verreries Feuquieres, Oise, France. Pressed glass perfume bottles, c. 1970s [A.N.V.]

S. A. V.

Smith & Chamberlin, Solar Works, Birmingham, Eng. Manufacturers of chandeliers and lustres. In use by about 1863. [Manley]

Jack Schmidt (b. 1947), U.S.A.   Glass
sculptures. [Grover]

SCHMIDT '70

Cristallerie Schneider, Epinay-sur-Seine,
France.   Established c. 1908 by Charles
Schneider, who studied under Gallé and
Daum. [Arwas/Schack]

Sig.: early period, acid etched

Early period, engraved

C. 1949-55, also with "à Paris" instead
of "France."

C. 1950-55, sandblasted signature of
designs by Robert Schneider, usually
under the base.

C. 1955-60 etched

C. 1960s to 1980s, applied with electri-
cal engraver.   May also include
"France."

A. C. Schonk, 18th c. Netherlands. Engraver in diamond point. [Weiss]

Signed work known.

Schott & Gen, Jena, Germany. Trademark registered c. 1904 in USA, but used before that date. [Peterson/Catalog]

Sig.: etched

Aert Schouman (1710-92), Holland. Stipple engraver; used English glasses. [Newman]

Signed work known.

Anna Marie van Schurmann (1607-1678), Netherlands. Calligraphic engraving in diamond point. [Weiss]

Signed work known.

Not identified. Probably USA, 20th century.

Sig.: molded on side of thimble box in form of cat.

William Manson's Glassworks, Scotland. Company established c. 1980. Paperweights. [Selman]

Trademark

Sig.: on bottom with thistle cane

Seattle Cut Glass Co., Seattle, Wash. Cutting shop, active 1917 to about 1922. [Revi]

Burtles, Tate & Co., Manchester, Eng.
Flint glass manufacturers.   Trade name
active circa 1895

Seneca Glass Co., Fostoria, Ohio.   Active
c. 1891-?.   Trademark active c. 1915.   Cut
glass of the Brilliant period. [JCK]

Seneca Glass Co., Morgantown, W. Va. Table
and gift wares, c. 1970s. [AGR]

Société   Anonyme   Chauffage   et   Eclairage
Sepulchre, Liege, Belgium.   Trademark re-
gistered   c. 1879.   Lighting   wares.
[Peterson]

Serica is a trade name; glass designed by
Copier,   designer   at   Leerdam   Glassworks,
Holland. See Leerdam. [Leerdam]

   Trademark

   Signed in diamond point

Verrerie   de   Sèvres, France.   Late 19th
century, produced art glass.   C. 1980s,

producing fine table wares. [Trademart/ Arwas]

Sig.: c. 1890s, on base

Sig. engraved and gilt, on four layer cameo vase with six cuttings, c. 1900.

Sèvres
1900

Script or block stenciled letters in circle, acid etched, c. 1980s.

Max Roland Erlacher (b. 1933), Corning, N.Y. After leaving Corning Glass Works, where he was an engraver, he opened his own studio. Trade name for lightly cut wares. [Farrar]

SHAMROC

Elizabeth Shrewsbury & Robert Howard, Birmingham, Eng. Glass manufacturers. Trademark active about 1876. [Manley]

United Glass Ltd., England. Trade name for machine pressed tumblers and other domestic tablewares. Active c. 1970s. [EGD]

SHERDLEY

Ennion, probably Sidon, Syria, first century A.D.

Sig.: Molded in glass. [Newman]

SIDON

Signet Glass Co., Corning, N.Y. c. 1913-1916. Brilliant cut glass. [Boggess/Farrar]

    Sig.: acid stamped

Chicago Heights Bottle Co., Chicago Heights, Ill. Trade name registered c. 1913. Used for bottles. [Peterson]

SIGNET

Silesia. Now a part of Czechoslovakia and Poland. [Blount]

    Sig.: Engraved on cameo vase.

Silesia

Huwer & Dannenhoffer, Brooklyn, N.Y. Trade name registered c. 1870s for lamp chimneys. Circa 1913, assigned to Silex Co., Malden, Mass. c. 1913. [Peterson]

SILEX

Deidrick Glass Co., Monaca, Pa. Patent process of silvered glass. Also attributed to be a name for brilliant cut glass. [Revi]

SILVART

    Forgeries are known.

La Bastie Glass Co., Ottawa, Ill. Trade name registered c. 1896, lighting wares. [Peterson]

SILVER

Silverbrook Art Glass, Riverhead, N.Y. Established 1946 by four Krentz brothers from Czechoslovakia. Maker of fancy clear glass animals.

    Paper label

"S G" surrounded by "SILVERBROOK ART GLASS"

See: Stevens & Williams. Type of art glass
with silver foil embedded between two
layers of glass, either clear or colored.
Circa 1900, developed by John Northwood II.
[Newman]

    Sig.: "England" may be added   SILVERIA

H. P. Sinclair & Co., Corning, N.Y. Circa
1904-28.

    Acid stamped block letters (about 8mm   SINCLAIR
    long) on tablewares. [Farrar]

Cristalleries de St. Louis, France. Prominent early glass manufacturer. In 1953,
resumed paperweight production with millefiori, lampwork, & sulphides. [Selman]

    Sig. on paperweights:

    Signature cane in red, blue or black

    Signed on back of sulphide in commemora-
    tion of centennial

    On same weight, on bottom

    Cane of red, blue or black. May also
    appear in reverse.

    Modern signature and date cane in
    paperweights

Sig.: etched on side of overlay vessel, probably 19th century

SLL. Not further identified. Engraved on cameo vase. May also be read SU (?). [Blount]

S. Maw, Son & Sons, London, England. Trademark registered c. 1871. Toilet articles.

L. E. Smith Glass Co., Mt. Pleasant, Pa. Established 1900's. Limited edition carnival glass plates first made in 1971.

Smith Brothers decorating shop, New Bedford, Mass. Arrived in America in 1855, worked for Mount Washington Glass Works as decorators. In 1871, left Mount Washington and formed their own business. Decorated imported opal glass blanks with fruit, flowers, orientalia, landscapes, etc. (Revi)

Sig.: fired enamel

Smith Bro's.

Paper label

Forgeries applied with acid etched stamp
or with black ink are reported [Cronin]

Samuel Mohn (1762–1815), Germany.   Worked
in Dresden from 1809; decorated tumblers
with city scenes, tourist sights, flowers,
and butterflies. First painter of silhouettes on china.   Developed transparent
enamels to replace opaque colors. Employed
apprentices and after 1809 used transfer
prints for outlines. After 1912, pieces
may also include signature of painter.
[Weiss]

S. MOHN FEC. 1812

Poth, Hille & Co., London.   Glass manufacturers.   Trademark   registered   1904.
[Manley]

Standard Oil Co. of New York.

   Sig.: trade name c. 1906

   Trademark circa 1914

SOCONY

Solar Prism Co., Cleveland, Ohio.   Circa
1899, glass tiles, etc. [Peterson]

Société Novelle des Verreries de L'Avesnois, Sonovera / Landrecies (Nord), France. Table services and crystal. Trade name active c. 1970s. [A.N.V.]

SONOVERA

Cristallerie et Verrerie de Vianne, Boulogne-sur-Seine, France. Commercial vases, crystal, etc. Trade name active c. 1970s.

SORBORNE

Verreries et Cristalleries de Souvigny, Souvigny, France. "Antique" glass, decorative items, table glass. Trade name active 1970s. [ANV]

SOUVIGNY-FRANCE

Izaak Spaan, 18th century, Netherlands. Engraver in diamond point. [Weiss]

Signed work known.

Max Ritter von Spaun (active 1879-1908), Bohemia. Grandson, or nephew according to another reference, of Johann Loetz; in 1908, became director of Loetz. Inspired by Louis Comfort Tiffany. [Arwas]

Sig.: Name wheel engraved, usually on items sold or given to museums.

Arrow device acid etched.

Livermore & Knight Co., Providence, R. I. Trade name registered circa 1907 for lighting items. [Peterson]

SPOOKIE SHADES

S. Schwartz. Active 1730 in Augsburg, Germany. Circa 1731, appointed court engraver to Prince Günther I of Schwarzburg-Sondershausen, Arnstadt, Thuringen. [Polak]

Südbayerische Sudetenglashütten, Kaufbeuren-Neugablonz, Germany. Trademark active c. 1970s, drink-wares. [Körting]

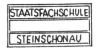

Industrial Trade School, Steinschönau, Bohemia. Established c. 1856. Paper label used c. 1911, Prof. Beckerta, director. [Nový]

Standard Cut Glass Co., N.Y. N.Y. Brilliant period cutting shop. Established before 1895. [Revi]

Star Crystal Co., W. Englewood, N.J. Table and gift wares, trademark active c. 1970s. [G & T]

Pabst & Esch, N.Y., N.Y. Trademark registered c. 1875, lighting items. [Peterson]

St. Clair Glass Works, Elwood, Ind. Established 1938. When Macbeth-Evans closed, John B. St. Clair (now out of work) started his own glassworks. Made replicas of Greentown glass. Closed, then reopened 1964. Gift wares. Limited edtion paperweights c. 1970s. [Kovel/Melvin]

Trademark die stamped in base of commercial grade paperweight.

ST. C.

Die stamped in base of paperweight while
glass is still soft; designed by Joe St.
Clair

paper label

Dominion Glass Co., Montreal, Can.   Active
c. 1970s. Maker of containers.

Trademark

ST. CLAIR

Legras et Cie.   Cameo vase with formal
plant forms with heavy gilt.   [Arwas/
Blount]

Sig.: on base in gilt, probably after
1909

Industrial Trade School, Steinschönau, Bohemia.   Organized in 1856 by Johann
Dvořaček. [Nový-Bor/Pazaurek]

Paper label used during Prof. Alfred
Dorna's directorship, c. 1919.

Sterling America.   Limited edition sterling
on crystal plates, introduced in 1970.
[Kovel]

Believed to be signed

Silver City Glass Co., Meriden, Conn. Trademark active c. 1970s. [G & T]

Sterling Glass Co., Cincinnati, Ohio. C. 1902-50. [Boggess/JCK]

Sig.: etched

Etched block letters

STERLING

Steuben Glass Works, Corning, N.Y. Established 1903 by Frederick Carder and Thomas Hawkes. Leading American maker of art glass. Acquired in 1918 by Corning Glass Works. After about 1933, only clear crystal items made. [Roberts/Gardner]

Sig.: art glass Aurene shades marked on inside of fitter rim, dusted with aluminum powder and fired. Letters are 3/8" to 1/2" high; fakes are larger.

Block letters also known on these shades. May be signed in diamond point.

STEUBEN

Be cautious of aluminum paint representing a rubbed signature.

Paper label of gold with embossed motif and lettering.

Acid stamped, after 1932.

Diamond point, after 1932:

S

Engraved on bottom in diamond point. Catalogue number may be omitted. "Aurene" registered in 1904.

Paper label with catalog number and price in ink:

Applied with rubber stamp, acid etched, used c. 1903-32, Fleur de lis 10.5 mm high. Beware of "S" that touches top of banner and the word "Steuben" with modern lettering.

Contemporary paper label

Stenciled mark on figural plaque [Auction].

STEUBEN C G W

Forgeries of most all marks exist.

Stevens & Williams, Brierley Hill, Stour-

bridge, England. Established 1819 by
Joseph Silvers and Joseph Stevens as Silvers Mills and Stevens. In 1847, became
Stevens and Williams when William Stevens
and Samuel Cox Williams, who both had
married daughters of Joseph Silvers, became
partners and sole owners. [Stevens &
Williams]

Sig.: cameo scent bottle c. 1887 with
silver mounts

STEVENS & WILLIAMS /
PATENT / ART GLASS/
STOURBRIDGE, ENGLAND

STEVENS & WILLIAMS 1901

STEVENS AND WILLIAMS LTD./
BRIERLEY HILL, J. MILLWARD

Factory mark under base, acid etched

Steven Mildwoff (b. 1940), USA. Independent sculptor.

STEVEN MILDWOFF

St. Gobain, Chauny & Cirey, Paris, France.
Maker of mirrors and lighting items.
Trademark registered 1895, label or etched.
[Peterson]

Compagnie des Cristalleries de St Louis, Münzthal, Lorraine. Wide range of fine crystal items up to present.

    Trademark

    Sig.: c. 1871-1918   ST LOUIS - MUNZTHAL

    Etched on cameo vase   ST LOUIS, NANCY

St. Ouen, France. [Blount]

    Sig.: engraved on cameo vase

L. Strauss & Son, N.Y., N.Y. Brilliant period cut glass, trademark registered c. 1894. [Revi/JCK]

    Sig.: Trademark not used as a signature.

    Forgeries known.

Strömberg Glass Works, Smaland, Sweden. Established c. 1933 by Edvard (1872-1946) & Gerda (d. 1960) Strömberg. He had been associated with Orrefors, Kosta, and Eda. From 1968 to 1977, produced limited edition plates, hand blown and cut. Produced other art wares. [Kovel/Newman]

    Sig.: engraved on base of vase, c. 1950   STROMBERG 942

Stuart & Sons, England.   Handmade crystal.
[Charlston]

    Trademark

Sig.: presentation goblet engraved by
David Peace (active 1975); also with his
trademark (style not known).

May also include: "England"

Incorrectly referenced as forged if the
mark does not read "Stuart's England."

Summit Art Glass Co., Mogadore, Ohio.
Pressed glass decorative items. Trademark
active c. 1980s.

General Electric Co., Schenectady, N.Y.
Trade name registered c. 1913 for lighting
wares. [Peterson]

SUNGLOW

Stevens & Williams, England. Lighting
wares. Trade name active c. 1970s. [DBC]

SUNGLOW

Sunkist.   Trade name for orange juice
products.

    Sig: molded in juicer, made about 1908.

SUNKIST

Macbeth-Evans, Pittsburgh, Pa. Fine flint
glass chimneys, same quality as Iron Clad,
but individually packed. [Price list]

Lighting Studios Co., N.Y., N.Y. Trade
name registered c. 1913. Lighting items.
[Peterson]

SUPERLUX

Susquehanna Glass Co., Columbia, Pa. Gift
wares, trademark active c. 1970s. [G & T]

Glashütte Süssmuth, Ger. Mouth-blown domestic ware. Trade name active c. 1970s.
[Körting]

SÜSSMUTHGLAS

Sven Palmqvist, Sweden. Designer at Orre-
fors since 1936. Developed "Ravenna,"
"Karak" ware, and other technical methods.
[Newman/Polak]

SVEN PALMQVIST

Stevens & Williams, England. [Stevens &
Williams]

   Sig.: Acid etched on cameo vase, c. 1910

C. 1924

Script with or without "England"   S & W ENGLAND

"K M," designer, Keith Murray (b. 1893),   S & W   K M
New Zealand architect who designed table
services and ornamental wares during the
1930s   of heavy   crystal   with   cut
decoration. [Stevens & Williams]

Sybren Valkema (b. 1916), Holland. Designer at Leerdam and co-director at Amsterdam School of Applied Arts.

Sig.: "0" is for 1966, each item marked
starting with "one" until end of year,
in diamond point on bottom.

Leerdam unica VO 122
Sybren Valkema

T

Willem Thibaut (1526-1599), Holland. Sixteenth century engraver and glass painter. [Gessert]

Tiffany Glass and Decorating Co., N.Y., N.Y., 1892-1902.   Established by Louis Comfort Tiffany. Leaded windows, art glass lamps, and vases.

> Trademark issued Nov. 13, 1894, used as a paper label embossed in green and gold or printed in black and white. May read "Favrile" or "Fabrile." Printed labels may have glass type between "Favrile" and "Glass," for example, "Sunset." This monogram was not used as an etched signature. [McKean]

Trademark   Paper label

Tiffany Glass Co., 1886-92, rare signature may be acid stamped in pontil. Beware of forgeries.

Tiffany Studios, N.Y., N.Y. Trademark registered c. 1904, but in use after 1902. See above. Paper label, not an acid stamp.

Tiffany & Co., N. Y., N. Y. Retail Jewelers, established in 1834 by father of Louis Comfort Tiffany. Mark used on wares from numerous sources retailed in the New York store.

Benjamin Lumsden Thomson, London. Enameler of decorative wares. Trademark registered about 1876. [Manley]

Cristallerie de Pantin. France. Moved to Pantin in 1855. Used on a cameo and enamel vase.

> Signed on base in gilt. C. 1855-1910 or later. [Arwas]

"T C P"

> Also, on same vessel

Thomas Wightman, Pittsburgh, Pa. Trademark for tablewares, stenciled, circa 1890s. [Peterson]

James or William Tassie, England. From 1766 made cameos of glass paste. See: Tassie. [Newman]

> Sig.: impressed

T

"T" not identified. Possibly a designer from the Wiener Werkstätte using Moser glass. Accompanied on European cameo vase by monogram of Moser of Carlsbad

Louis Comfort Tiffany.

    Sig.: wheel cut on iridescent art glass
vase. [Neuwirth]
Questionable if this is a Tiffany
signature.

                                                                   03363

Victor Trabucco, Buffalo, N.Y. Since 1977,
making paperweights in editions of 25 to
75. Fish, flowers, etc.

    Sig.: in cane. Signature and date   T
etched on side. [Selman]

James L. Tanner (b. 1941), U.S.A. Sculptor
and instructor.

    Sig.: may also include title   TANNER '71

Tapio Wirkkala (b. 1915). From 1947 designer at Karhula, Iittala, Finland. Also
designed for Venini, Murano, Italy.
[Newman/Polak]

    Sig.: diamond point on pieces of his   TAPIO WIRKKALA /
designs. Full name possibly added   VENINI/ITALIA /
later. [Auction]   T W / 1968

                       TAPIO WIRKKALA - IIITALA

Stevens & Williams, England. Trade name
registered 1886. [Manley]   TAPESTRY GLASSWARE

James Tassie (1735-99) and nephew William
Tassie (1777-1860), England. From 1766
made reproductions of antique engraved gems
in white and colored glass paste. [Wills]

    Sig.: impressed   TASSIE

Taylor Bros. Co. Philadelphia, Pa. Established 1902, closed 1915 by bankruptcy. Fine quality cut glass of the brilliant style. [Revi]

Sig.: acid etched

Other reported signature

TAYLOR BROTHERS

T. Baillie & Co., London. Maker of stained glass. Trademark registered 1888. [Manely]

Herberts Decorative Glass Works, London. Decorating studio. Trademark registered 1910. [Manley]

T. Fall, England, circa 1880s-90s. Victorian topographical painter. [Manley]

Sig.: on painted opal ware

T. FALL

Thomas (1849-1926) and George (1850-1925) Woodall, England. Cameo carvers, worked at Thomas Webb & Sons. [Grover/Thos. Webb & Co.]

Sig.: 1880-1900

J & G Woodall

J & G Woodall

T & G WOODALL/WEBB & SONS/GEM CAMEO

T & G WOODALL/WEBB/with title

T & G WOODALL/ DES. & SCULP./THOMAS WEBB & SONS/GEM CAMEO

Thatcher Bros. and Thatcher Bros. & Co., Fairhaven and later Falmouth, Mass. In 1886, bought out cutting shop of Smith Brothers of New Bedford, Mass. Trademark used from 1894, closed in 1907. [Revi]

Sig.: label printed in red ink.

Theodore B. Starr, N.Y. Retailer of fine goods, circa 1900-1924. [Auction]

Sig.: etched on base of cameo vase

THEODORE B. STAR /
NEW YORK

Theresienthaler Krystallglas Fabrik, Bayern, Germany. Stemware. Trademark active c. 1970s. [Körting]

Thiancourt. France. Possibly designer at Pantin during the 19th century. Usually floral designs, acid cut with some carving. [Arwas/Hilschenz]

Sig.: script under base, also with number such as "11"

Same piece also engraved "Schneider"

George J. Thiewes (b. 1943), U.S.A.
Sculptures.

    Sig.: includes title and date. [Grover]   THIEWES 1971

Thomas Webb & Sons: John Shepherd & Thos.
Webb at White House Glassworks 1833-40;
Thos. Webb's glassworks "The Flats,"
1840-1855;
Thos. Webb, Dennis Glass Works, 1835-1859;
Thos. Webb & Sons, Dennis Glass Works, 1859
on. [Thos. Webb & Co./Grover]

    Sig.: engraved on cameo work   THOS. WEBB & SONS, Lᴛᴅ.

Circular acid stamp on intaglio and   THOMAS WEBB & SONS /
cameo vase, circa 1900.   GEM CAMEO

September 1980 on, sandblasted   THOMAS
WEBB
ENGLAND

Aug. 1966 to Aug. 1980, sandblasted   THOS
WEBB
ENGLAND

Acid etched on Burmese glass ware   QUEEN'S BURMESE WARE / THOS. WEBB & SONS / PATENTED / Rᵈ 88167

Other signatures on cameo pieces. THOMAS WEBB & SONS/

GEM CAMEO/PARIS EXHIBITION 1889

THOMAS WEBB & SONS GEM CAMEO/
T HUDSON

THOMAS WEBB & SONS/GEM CAMEO/
TIFFANY & CO.
PARIS EXHIBITION 1889

THOS. WEBB & SONS

Thomire, Paris, France, circa 1840s.

   Sig.: signed on cut glass box [Auction]   THOMIRE à PARIS

Wm. R. Noe, N.Y., N.Y. Lighting items.
Trademark circa 1890s. [Peterson]

Three Feather Brand

Thomas Hudson, Newcastle, England. Copper
wheel engraving. Active circa 1840s. See   T. HUDSON
Thomas Webb. [Wakefield]

Mook et Bole, 60 Rue Ordener, Paris.

   Sig.: used on art deco glass lamp shade,   TIANY
   painted with Dutch scene, circa early
   20th century. [Catalogue]

Tiffany Glass Co., c. 1886-1892.
Tiffany Glass & Decorating Co., 1892-1902.
Tiffany Studios, after 1902.

Established by Louis Comfort Tiffany, sold
to A. Douglas Nash in 1928. Leading maker
of art glass, leaded lamp shades and leaded
windows. [McKean]

Earliest paper label without monogram.

TIFFANY FABRILE

or

TIFFANY FAVRILE

Paper label (see monogram section.)

Leaded windows from 1890 to 1899,
usually signed in lower right corner in
black enamel or acid stamped on piece of
flashed glass, leaded in. Signature
form most often used:

TIFFANY GLASS & DECORATING COMPANY
NEW YORK

Leaded windows 1892-1902, often included
address on separate piece of glass
leaded into corner.

TIFFANY GLASS & DECORATING CO.
333-341 4th AVENUE, NEW YORK

Leaded window: "Feeding the Flamin-
goes," before 1902, signed in enamel.

TIFFANY GLASS & DEC. CO./
333-341 4th AVE. N.Y.

Rare signature on windows circa
1890-1899, giving copyright date

COPYRIGHT 1896
TIFFANY GLASS & DECORATING COMPANY
NEW YORK

After 1902 to about 1915, block letters
become common on leaded windows. May
include date.

TIFFANY STUDIOS
NEW YORK

Rare signature form, circa 1905

Leaded lamp shades, before 1902, signature impressed on narrow copper strips and soldered to inside of rim, often with design number. Patinated as shade. May be three separate strips.

TIFFANY STUDIOS   NEW YORK   1529-4

Lampshade: after 1902, impressed on plate soldered to shade rim. Sometimes includes number of pattern design.

TIFFANY STUDIOS
NEW YORK

TIFFANY STVDIOS
NEW YORK

21667

Impressed under foot of bronze lamp base

TIFFANY & CO.
PARIS EXHIBITION 1889

used on exhibition pieces. Other cities and dates are similarly noted

Note: Vessels, lamp shades, and other objects made by Steuben, Imperial, Paul Crist Studios, etc. may bear forged Tiffany signatures. Study form and metal. Acid etched signatures, other than the rare monogram, are not authentic.

Other signatures see: "L" section and monogram sections.

United States Glass Co., Pittsburgh, Pa. Cut glass early 20th century. Tiffin Glass

Co., subsidiary of Continental Can Co., Tiffin, Ohio, table and gift ware. Trademark active circa 1960s. Successors to United States Glass Co. trade name.

Peerless Lead Glass Works, Ellwood City, Pa., circa 1890s, for lighting wares. [Peterson]

TIGER BRAND/OIL FINISH/
FINE FLINT/
with head of a tiger

Timo Sarpaneva (b. 1926), Finland. Designer at Iittala since 1950. [Polak]

Sig.: engraved on every piece made to his design.

TIMO SARPANEVA IITTALIA

Tischler. Not further identified. Used on vase with enameled painting of a bird. Circa 1900. [Auction]

Sig.: acid stamped on underside of vase   TISCHLER

Also, on same piece a horseshoe enclosing "R F" in monogram.

John Robinson, Stourbridge Flint Glass Works, Pittsburgh, Pa. C. 1823-35. Pressed wares. [Islin]

T & J ROBINSON PITTSB^G

Jindrich Tockstein (b. 1914), Czech. [Grover]

Signed on sculptural form with engraving. May include title and date.   TOCKSTEIN

A "Trade Mark" is a protected design, registered with the proper government agency to protect its owner from unauthorized use. The symbol may be used exclusively by that company to mark its products.

TRADEMARK

It has been reported to be applied to some ware without specific meaning in order to make them appear important. [Cronin]

Stourbridge Glass Co. Ltd., Britain. Trade name for cut lead crystal tablewares. Active 1970s. [DBG]

Trade name

TUDOR CRYSTAL

Sig.: etched on foot of rock-crystal style stemware

TUDOR

Tuthill Cut Glass Co., Middletown, N. Y. C. 1900-23, cutting shop of very fine quality brilliant cut glass. [Revi/Daniels]

Sig.: etched

Known accompanied by a stylized fish. [Boggess]

T. Vinards. Limited edition sculptures and plates, circa 1980s. [Merchandise Mart]

Sig.: diamond point on base.

T. VINARDS

Thomas Woodall, 19th century, England. See Thomas Webb.

Sig.: on rock crystal style vase

T. WOODALL

Steuben Glass Works.   Rare style of art
glass developed by Frederick Carder, circa
1916-17.   A change in temperature during
manufacture alters its color from blue-
green to Tyrian purple.

   Sig.: on base of vase   TYRIAN

U

United States Glass Co. Pittsburgh, Pa.
Cut glass and other wares. Depression
glass c. 1920s-30s. Trademark registered
after 1914. [Weatherman/Revi]

    Sig.: molded

Unger Brothers, Newark, N.J. C. 1901-18.
Cutting shop for brilliant cut glass.
[Revi/Boggess]

    Trademark.

    Signed: etched

Universal Glass Products Co., Parkersburg,
W. Va. Trademark active c. 1970s. [AGR]

Union Glass Co., Sommeville, Mass. Circa
1851-1927. Established by Amory Houghton.
Brilliant cut glass maker and cutting
shop. [Boggess]

    Sig.: stamped on metal liner for a cut
    glass ferner.

U G C O

U G CO / SOMMERVILLE

Universal Glass Products Co., Parkersburg,
W. Va. Trademark active c. 1970s. [AGR]

UGP

Van der Hoef, Europe. Jungenstil designs.
Not further identified. [Gysling-Billeter]

Untw. v. d. Hoef

Unger Bros., Newark, N.J. Cutting shop for
brilliant cut glass, 1901–18. [Boggess]

   Sig.: etched

**UNGER
BROS**

United States Glass Co., Pittsburgh, Pa.

   Sig.: molded on depression glass wares.
   [Weatherman]

U. S. G. CO. /
PATENT PENDING

V

Marianne v. Allesch (b. 1886), Germany. Moved to U. S. A. during the war. [Polak]

Vereinigte Glasfabriken, Leerdam, Holland. Since 1968. See: Leerdam. [Van der Meer]

Val St. Lambert, Belgium. [Klesse/Mayr]

Sig.: Cameo on cameo vase, c. 1906 [Klesse/Mayr]

In blue inlay under foot of vase with overlay decoration c 1920

Compagnia Venezia & Murano, Glass Works, Murano, Italy. Established by Antonio Salviati in 1877. [Newman]

Lancaster Glass Corp., Lancaster, Ohio. Trademark active 1970s. [AGR]

Summit Art Glass Co., Mogadore, Ohio. Trademark active 1980s. Gift wares. [Price list]

Monongahela Valley Cut Glass Co. Gift wares. Trademark active c. 1970s. [G&T]

Vallérysthal Glass Works, established 1836, as subsidiary of Plaine de Walsch Glass Works. Amalgamated into Société des Verreries Réunies de Plaine de Walsch et Vallérysthal in 1854. In 1855, became Klenglin et Cie when Société des Verreries Réunies de Plaine de Walsch et Vallérysthal disolved. For a brief time at the end of the 19th century, produced art glass including an iridescent type. Also, large producer of fine tableware. [Taub]

Sig.: engraved in diamond point in various leaf forms in pontil of base, usually gilt.

Other signature forms:

Vallery st thal

Vallarysthal   **VALLERYSTHAL**

Cristalleries du Val-Saint-Lambert, Liége, Belgium. Established 1825, still largest glass works in Belgium. Art glass and fine useful wares. [Broham/Arwas]

Trademark: acid etched on Art Deco vase circa 1920s.

Paper label

327

Sig.: a wide variety of styles:

Engraved on cameo vase

Signature of copper deposit on vase with
blue enamel

Val St Lambert

BELGIQUE

Signed in enamel on cameo and enameled
vessel

Signed on cameo and intaglio vessel   VAL ST. LAMBERT 128,
designed by George Graffart   GRAFFART

Signed with Samuel J. Herman's initials
on iridescent vase streaked with pads
and pulls

Signed in diamond point underfoot;   VAL ST LAMBERT / LL SJH
artists' initials: Louis Le Loup and S.
J. Herman

Since 1968, acid etched on limited   VAL ST. LAMBERT
edition plates

Van Bull, 18th century Netherlands. Engraver in diamond point.

Signed work known.

Vandermark Merritt. C. 1980s.

   Sig.: molded on base of cameo vase

VANDERMARK MERRITT

   etched on scent bottles

VANDERMARK

Van Heusen, Charles & Co., Albany, N.Y.
1864-1945. Retailers of cut glass. [Revi]

   Sig.: etched

E. J. S. Van Houten, New York, N. Y.
Cutting shop for brilliant cut glass,
active 1896-1919. [Revi]

Cristalleries de Vannes-le-Châtel, Meurthe,
France. Table services, stemware, and orna-
mentals. Active 1960 to present

   Etched on bottom of molded animal

   Some ware may state "fabrication main"
   (handmade).

   Sig.: Etched on stemware

   Etched on stemware

VANNES-LE-CHÂTEL

Van Son.   Limited edition paperweights,   Known to be signed
c. 1972. [Kovel]

Varnish & Co., London, England.   Patent
process for sealing silver within a double-
walled vessel. C. 1850s. [Grover/Wills]

   Sig.: metallic disk, about $\frac{1}{2}$" diameter,   VARNISH & CO. PATENT / LONDON
   imbedded in foot of a glass.   VARNISH & CO.

Strathearn Glass Co., Vasart Glass Ltd.,
Scotland.   Hand blown vases of mottled
colors, cluthra, etc.   Trade name active
1970s. [Manley/Selman]

   Sig.: on base of vessel with rough wheel   *Vasart*
   engraving

Louis F. Vaupel (1824–1903), U.S.A.   Engraver at the New England Glass Co. from
1853 to 1885.   After that he practiced
wheel engraving at his home. [Fauster]

   Sig.: a wine glass, possibly a trial   VAUPEL/239
   piece.   LT-CH PATTERN/NO 43

Veles.   Not identified, probably France
c. 1905–10.   Art Noveau style.   Two layer
cameo etched in relief on side of vessel.   **VELES**
[Venzmer]

Fostoria Glass Specialty Co., Fostoria,   VELURIA
Ohio.   Trade name registered 1911. [Peter-
son]

Vemçomy.   Vase with Art Deco design.   Not
further identified.   [Auction]

Vemçomy

Venini Glassworks, Murano, Italy.   Established c. 1925 by Paolo Venini (b. 1895).
Presently operated by his descendants.
Revived old Venetian glass working methods,
such as millefiori and filigrana, and
developed new ones.   [Polak]

   Sig.: engraved or acid stamped.   May
   have "Made in Italy" instead of
   "Italia."

venini
mmrano
ITALIA

   Ludovico Diaz De Santillana, designer.

VENINI / ITALIA / LDS 1959/
LUDOVICO DIAZ DE SANTILLANA

   Tapio Wirkkala, Finnish designer, who
   served as art director.   Diamond point.

VENINI ITALIA / TW 1969/

TAPIO WIRKKALA -

Verame. Not identified. [Auction]

   Sig.: molded into bowl decorated with
   acid cutback design.

VERAME

Florence Talbot, Westbrook, San Francisco,
Calif.   Circa 1912, trade name for handpainted wares. [Peterson]

VERKO

Société des Verreries/Sarrebourg, France.
Fine crystal stemware and decorative items.
Trade name active c. 1970s. [ANV]

VERLOR

Verlys Glass, France.   Frosted silky
glass, blown or molded.   From 1955-57,
molds were used by Heisey.

   Sig.: Heisey licensee, paper label or
   diamond point.

   An engraved or molded script without
   "France" suggests Heisey's American
   production.
   Used on a molded bowl

   Some state that American ware was marked
   only with paper labels, but some author-
   ities dispute this statement.

Verlys

Henry Symes & Co., Brighton, England.
Tradename registered about 1907. [Manely]

VERRADIANT

Vernons Patent China & Glass Co., London.
Retailers.   Trademark registered about
1883. [Manley]

Verreries de Lorraine, France.   Glass
designed by Désiré Christian. [Taub]

   Signature used circa 1900 on items
   exhibited at Paris World Exhibition.

Charles Vessière, Nancy.   Designer about
1900 at Baccarat.

   Sig.: engraved under foot of bowl with
   irregular rim, made of green glass with
   iridescence.

Vessière Baccarat Nancy

Eska Mfg. Co., Baltimore, Md.   Cut glass
trade name. [Revi]

VESTALIA

John Walsh Walsh, Soho & Vesta Glass Works,
Brimingham, England.   Trade name registered
about 1907. [Manley]

VESTA VENETIAN

Victory Glass Inc., Jeannette, Pa.   Decorative items.   Trademark active c. 1970s.
Maker of milk glass. [AGR]

Viking Glass Co., New Martinsville, W. Va.
Trademark active c. 1970s, table and gift
wares. [G&T]

Villeroy & Boch, Germany.   In 1842, established glass factory at Wadgassen.   Circa
1902-34, produced 2-layer acid etched cameo
designs   of   floral   and   plant   motifs.
[Arwas]

    Sig.: designed by E. Rigot, signed in
    cameo.

VILLEROY & BOCH /
E. RIGOT

Wiesenthal Crystal, Germany.   Trade name
for table and gift ware active c. 1970s.

VISTRA CRYSTAL

Cristallerie et Verrerie de Vianne,
Boulogne-sur-Seine, France.   Vases, domestic and commercial wares.   Trade name
active c. 1970s. [ANV]

VITOUVER

Victoria Mansions, Westminster, England. Glass manufacturer. Trade name in use about 1884.

VITRITE

Anchor Hocking Glass Company, USA. Early 20th century depression glass. [Florence]

VITROCK

Otto Vittali (1872-1919), France. In 1905, began to decorate glass with opaque enamel and gold and silver. [Hilschenz]

Vladimir Jelinek (b. 1934), Bohemia. Designer of wide range of decorative items and sculptures.

V. JELINEK / 1971

Věra Lišková, Prague. Active 1967. Lamp work vessel. [Kessel/Mayr]

Sig.: diamond point on foot

Venice & Murano Glass & Mosaic Co., Ltd. Succeeded by Pauley & Co., Venice.

Sig.: used on cameo vase prior to 1900

Société Française de Verrerie Mecanique Champenoise, Reims, France. Stemware and decorative items. Trademark active c. 1900.

V. M. C.

Verrerie de Sèvres, France. Circa 1885,
became Cristalleries de Sèvres et Clichy
Réunis. End of the nineteenth and early
twentieth centuries, produced art glass
inspired by the Art Nouveau movement.
[Arwas]

Sig.: etched on bottom

On same vase in cameo on side: LORRAINE

See: Val St. Lambert.

Sig.: cameo and intaglio vase with cameo
signature. George Graffart became head
of design department from 1942 to 1958.

Graffart's design executed by factory   V
craftsman

Graffart's design executed at Val Glass   EV
School

Graffart's engraved designs   "C G" and design number

Circa 1925, label denoting pieces by Val   A. D. P.
St. Lambert exhibited at Arts Decoratifs
Exhibition, Paris.

Signatures of this style attributed to
pieces designed by Henry Muller and his
brother, circa 1906

Vally Wieselthier (d. 1943). Designer at
the Wiener Werkstätte. Migrated to U.S.A.
in 1929. [Auction]

Sig.: in enamel on enamel decorated bowl   V. WIESELTHIER

On same bowl, Wiener Werkstätte monogram

W

Wolfgang Buhler (active 1588–1611). Glass window painter. [Gessert]

R. Williamson & Co., Chicago, Ill. Lighting ware. Trademark in use circa 1920s. [Catalogue]

Westite (c. 1930s). U.S.A. Attributed to Akro Agate [Florence]

Maker not identified. Possibly Austrian circa 1910.

Sig.: on a pokal decorated with engraving.

Presumed to be mark of a Birmingham, England, die maker working about 1839. Initial is placed under the portrait bust on a commemorative pressed glass plate dated 1839. [Wakefield]

Westmoreland Glass Co., Grapeville, Pa. Trademark registered circa 1910; still in operation. Pressed glass table and decorative wares.

Sig.: molded

Francis Dyer Whittemore, Jr. (b. 1921), Landsdale, Pa. First limited edition paperweights made in 1968. [Cloak/Selman]

Sig.: in cane underneath or at edge of design; in rose weights at the junction of leaves and rose.

Wood Brothers Glass Co., Ltd., Barnsley, Eng. High-quality toilet and perfume ware and industrial products. Trademark active circa 1960s. [DBG]

Sig.: molded

Wallace Silver Co., Wallingford, Conn. Limited edition crystal sculptures beginning in 1974. [Kovel]

Believed to be signed

Villeroy and Boch, Wadgassen, Germany.

Sig.: etched

Almeric Walter (1859-1942), Nancy, France.

Sig.: molded in pâte de verre. [Arwas]

Waterford Crystal Ltd., Waterford, Ireland. Opened in 1951. Has no relation to "antique Waterford" mentioned in historical glass surveys. Maker of good quality stemware, lamps, etc. [Newman]

Trademark

Sig.: block or Gothic letters etched on bottom of items.

Waterloo Co., Cork, Ireland. Circa 1815. Decanters. [Davis]

Sig.: molded in base

WATERLOO CO / CORK

Watson Brothers, Calgary, Alberta, Canada. Brilliant style cut glass. [Boggess]

WATSON BROTHERS

C. F. Monroe Co., Meriden, Conn. Trade name for opal glassware, usually decorated with florals in pastel enamels. Registered circa 1892. [Revi/Grimmer]

Sig.: printed and fired brown/pink or black ink.

TRADE WAVE MARK
CREST

Printed and fired brown/pink

Paper labels

Webb • Corbett Ltd., Stourbridge, Eng. Conveyed, in 1897, to Thomas Webb III (1865-1925) and Corbett. The name, Webb-Corbett, Ltd., adopted in the 1930s. In 1969, became part of the Royal Doulton Group. [Newman/Manley]

    Sig.: used on spatter ware vase.   W & C

Colen Mayers Ltd., England. Cut crystal wares. Trade name active circa 1970s.   WEALDEN CRYSTAL

Thomas Webb & Sons, England. Art glass of the 19th century. [Thos. Webb Crystal/ Wakefield]

    Sig.: 1889-1905, Registered #87918, etched.

1906-1935, acid etched

1936-1949, acid etched

1950-July 1966, acid etched

Many dubious signatures exist that are not consistent with the quality of Webb's works.

Webb-Corbett, Ltd. England. Handmade and hand-decorated full lead crystal for domestic use.

Trademark registered 1897.

Modern mark with "S" for the Stourbridge factory and "T" for the Tutbury factory [Western Collector]

Acid etched. Attributed to Webb.

WEBBS
IRIS
GLASS

Trade name active circa 1970s.

WEBB CORBETT CRYSTAL

Block letters on lead crystal tablewares, circa 1970s.

WEBB

Samuel Clarke, London. Candlemaker and developer of night light candle. Trade name registered about 1887. [Manley]

WEE – FAIRY

Emil Rudolf Weiss (b. 1875), Germany. From 1970-33, instructor at the school attached to the Arts & Crafts Museum and to the United States School for Pure and Applied Art, both located in Berlin. [Arwas]

Sig.: in cameo of industrial Gallé style cameo ware.

Dema Glass Ltd., England. Trade name active circa 1970s for drinkware. [DBG]

WELLINGTON

Welsbach Co., Gloucester, N.J. Trademark active 1904, for lamp chimneys. [Catalogue]

TRADE

WELSBACH

MARK

C. A. F. Werther, Cologne, Ger. Diamond point engraver. Mid-eighteenth century. [Weiss]

Signed work known.

Western Sand Blast Co., 1876–1920. Western Sandblast Mfg. Co., since 1920. Chicago. Maker of sand blasted designs on doors and windows, leaded art glass windows and doors for church, residence, and advertising. [Darling]

    Sig.: sandblasted on base of door light

WESTERN SAND BLAST CO / CHICAGO

Westmoreland Glass Co., Grapeville, Pa. Trademark registered circa 1910. Table and decorative items. Limited edition plates since 1972, handpainted in gold on black glass.

    Paper label

West Virginia Glass Specialty Co., Weston, W. Va. Table and gift wares. Trademark active 1970s.

William Fritsche. Bohemian glass worker at Dennis Glass Works of Thomas Webb & Sons, Eng. Circa 1878, introduced rock-crystal engraving at the Paris Exposition. [Wakefield]

W FRITSCHE

Wheaton Industries, Millville, N.J. Hand blown and pressed decorative wares. Limited edition plates since 1971. [Kovel]

Trademark.:

C. E. Wheelock & Co., Peoria, Ill. Trademark used since 1898. Wholesalers and retailers of cut glass. Still in business in 1964. [Revi]

Sig.: label or etched

J. W. Tobin, N.Y., N.Y. Trade name registered circa 1909, lighting items. [Peterson]

WHICHWAY

Whitall, Tatum & Co., Philadelphia, Pa. & N.Y., N.Y. Established circa 1857. Became part of Armstrong Cork Co. in 1938. Made translucent milk glass apothecary wares. [McKearin]

Sig.: molded in a small circle

WHITALL TATUM & CO./
PHILA. & N.Y.

Gill Brothers Co., Steubenville, Ohio. Lighting wares. Trade name registered 1884. [Peterson]

    Sig.: printed on label or etched   WHITE STAR

New England Glass Works, East Cambridge, Mass. Trade name for a shaded peach-colored ware. Registered circa 1886. [Fauster]

    Sig.: paper label

Wilhelm Kralik Sohn, Bohemia. From 1899, made iridescent glass and cameo wares. Closed during World War II. [Arwas/Klesse]

    Sig.: in cameo or acid etched with stencils on side of vessel   WILHELM KRALIK SOHN / BOHEMIA

Wilhelm von Eiff (1890-1943), Stuttgart, Ger. Worked with Lalique and Lobmeyr (c. 1921). Taught at Stuttgart Trade School. Also worked with Württembergische Metallwarenfabrik (WMF). Circa 1920s and 1930s, engraved in "Hochschnitt." Circa 1930s, invented a hand-held tool for engraving windows. [Polak]

    Sig.: engraved on goblet   WILHELM VON EIFF

Willem Fortuijn, 17th century, Netherlands. Engraver in diamond point and stipple. [Weiss]   Signed work known.

William Leighton. Patentee of process developed by E. Varnish & Co. for silvered glass, c. 1855. [Revi]

    Sig.: below plug that seals hole where silver is inserted.   WILLIAM LEIGHTON

William Manson, Glasgow, Scotland. Since 1979, maker of paperweights with reptiles, fish, and floral motifs.

    Sig.: signature and date cane and numbered on base   WILLIAM MANSON

Iorio Glass Shop, Flemington, N. J. Established by William J. Iorio, son of Louis, who worked at Empire Cut Glass Co. Since 1966, making lampwork paperweights. [Melvin]

    Sig.: acid etched   W. IORIO 1969

Tapio Wirkkala, Finland. Designer at Iittala Glassworks, Finland. Working about 1947. Sculptures. [Grover/Polak]   WIRKKALA

Willem Jacobz van Heemskerk (1613–1692), Leyden, Netherlands. Decorator in stipple; often engraved calligraphy on green bottles, römmers, and dishes. [Weiss]

    Sig.: in diamond point   W. J. V. HEEMSKERK 1683
    Some pieces may be dated.

W. J. Wilson, England. Commemorative glass, circa 1940. [Exhibition item]

    Sig.: on pontil   W. J. WILSON

Wenzel Kulka Glassworks, Haida, Czech. [Pazaurek]

Willem Mooleyser (active 1685-97), Rotterdam. Engraver in diamond point on bowls, flasks, goblets, etc. [Newman]

Sig.: some are dated   W M

Württembergische Metallwarenfabrik, Stuttgart, Ger. Steelworks established 1855; glass works established circa 1883. Most wares not signed. [Schwandt]

Paper label with "Ikora" or "Myra."

"Ikora" and "Lavaluna" glass often have pattern or experiment number scratched or cut on base

Karl Wiedmann (b. 1905). Designer at WMF from 1925 to 1927. Signed in diamond point. This engraved signature with full name was applied during the 1970s to pieces from his private collection.

Etched on stemware c. 1980s

                    WMF

On silverplated fittings; "B" for Britannia metal.   W M F B

William Northwood (1858-1937), nephew of
John, produced cameo pieces by hand at
Stevens and Williams, England, 19th cen-
tury. [Beard]

W. NORTHWOOD

George (1830-1925) and Thomas (1849-1926)
Woodall.   Outstanding cameo carvers at
Thomas Webb and Sons.   Thomas retired in
1911. [Grover/Beard]

   Sig.:

Woodall

Woodall

Woodall

Wilhelm Otto Robart (1696-1778), The
Hague. [Weiss]

W: O: R

Attributed to William Reading, a Birmingham, England, die maker, working about
1828.

   Sig.: Molded in border of commemorative
   lacy pressed glass plate. [Wakefield]

WR

Wright Rich Cut Glass, Anderson, Ind.
Maker of medium quality cut glass during
the brilliant period. Trademark active
1904, out of use by 1915. [Revi/JCK]

Tmk.:

Sig.: etched

W. Stuurman (b. 1908). Designer of animal
figures. At Leersdam until 1945. [Van der
Meer]

W. Steinbeck, possibly Bohemia, mid-
nineteenth century.

Sig.: inscribed in diamond point of side
of tumbler in the Biedermeier style.

W. STEINBECK

Professor Wilhelm von Eiff (1890-1943).
Professor at Stuttgart Trade School, Ger-
many. At Lobmeyr's c. 1920s. Engraver.
[Pazaurek/Arwas]

W.v. E

W
v
Eiff.

Wiener Werkstätte, Austria. Active from
1911 to 1932, produced mostly "Jugendstill"
designs. [Arwas]

Sig.; etched on finial of covered vase
in the Art Deco style. Usually accompanied by designer's initials.

Another monogram form, acid etched

Not further identified. Attributed to Germany or Bohemia c. 1900.

    Sig.: in enamel on enamel decorated goblet [Venzmer]

X

Harry Caralluzzo, Toledo, Ohio. Circa
1980's, magnum sized footed paperweights
with roses made with crimps.

    Used on later pieces the mark is at   X
    pontil breakoff on the bottom.

Z

F. Zitzmann (1840-1906), Steinach, Germany. Glassblower, lampworker, and designer at Ehrenfeld. [Pazaurek]

$\mathcal{Z}$

Zimmerman Art Glass Co., Corydon, Ind. Established in 1953. Paperweights by Joseph Zimmerman. [Melvin/Cloak]

    Sig.: copper wire impressed into base   Z

    Die mark molded on base while metal is still soft   Z

    Paper labels

Joseph A. Morrell, Baton Rouge, La. Master blower, designer and owner of Zellique Art Glass, established about 1980. Tiffany-style iridescent art glass, c. 1980's. [Merchandise Mart]

    Sig.: engraved on base of art glass vessels.   ZELLIQUE

Macbeth-Evans Glass Co., Pittsburgh, Pa. Trademark registered c. 1895 for top quality lead glass lamp chimneys. [Catalog]

    Sig.: etched

Zeuner (active 1773-1810), Amsterdam. Engraver of panels and objects using an élomisé style. Gold and silver leaf, often with colored field. [Newman]

Signed work known.

Glossary

Translations of Selected Foreign Words

Atelier: studio

Bleikristal: lead crystal

Chinoiserie: Chinese-like

Cire perdue: lost wax casting method

Cristallerie: crystal manufactory

et Cie.: and Company

Etablissement: establishment, business

Fachschule: trade school

Frères: brothers

Gebrüder: brothers

Glashütte: glassworks

Glashüttenwerke: glassworks (glass-house works)

Glasmanufaktur: glass manufacturer

Grisaille, en: painted in tones of gray

Hochschnitt: engraved in high relief

Intaglio: engraved with design below surface of body

Jugendstil: Germanic decorative style, circa early 1900s.
Literally translated, the young style. Has elements of both Art Nouveau and Art Deco.

Kunstgewerbeschule: art school

Kunsthandwerk: art handwork

Kunstindustrieschule: industrial arts school

Laub-und-bandelwerk: strapwork and foliage design

Pâte de verre: glass paste

Réunis: amalgamated

Römer: Germanic style wine glass with globular bowl and spread hollow stem

Schwarzlot: painting in black

Société anonyme: incorporated

Staat: government

Tiefschnitt: deeply engraved, intaglio

Verrerie: glassworks

Verrier: glassworker

Werkstätte: workshop

Zwischengold: design of gold applied between layers of clear glass.

Benchmark Dates
Technical and Historical

Seventeenth Century

1668   Cast plate glass first made in St. Gobain, France.

1674   Ravenscroft granted patent for crystal.

1676   Ravenscroft first uses lead oxide to produce glass.

1687   Tischirnhaus and Böttger set up engraving and polishing mill for glass on the Weissenritz River (Germany).

1690-91 Friedrich Winter at Petersdorf uses water power for engraving.

1615   England prohibits use of wood for glass furnaces. Shipbuilding industry jeopardized by shortage of wood. Glasshouses move away from forests of the south to coalfields of Midlands.

Eighteenth Century

Natural sodium sulphate (improved soda) discovered in Siberia. Tints glass amber.

Improved soda (sodium sulphate) reduced with coal.

1725-30 Nickel added as decolorizer in England. Green tint of glass changes to gray.

1740s   Manganese in use in England as decolorizer. Lighter tint of glass.

1750   Rottenstone introduced for polishing. Smear marks disappear.

by 1764 Lead in use in at least one French glassworks.

1773   Cast plate introduced into England.

1775   Price of Barilla high. French Academy offers prize for process to produce soda from common table salt.

1777-78 Steam power is introduced in England.

1787   Nicolas Lebanc refines soda from sea salt (black ash). Method used for fifty years.

1792   Richard Murdoch distills gas from coal (Cornwall). Establishes gas as a light source.

1798   First Paris International Trade Exposition.

1798   Napoleon's Egyptian campaign.

Nineteenth Century

c. 1800 In France glassworkers change from potash to soda made from marine plant alkali (Spanish Barilla). Better quality glass, but greenish or bluish tint.

c. 1800 Potash from burned wood used for flux.

1816   Robert Stirling patents glass furnace heated by regenerative process.

Baccarat introduces lead.

by 1820 Pressing introduced using side lever, hand-operated press.

Three- and four-piece hardwood glass pressing molds replaced by brass, copper, and cast iron molds.

1820   Charles Chubsea (Stourbridge) devises iron mold that folds together and opens automatically.

1820	Gas in use in U.S. for lighting.
1821	Blowing with air pressure pump invented at Baccarat.
1825	First U.S. patent for pressed glass is issued to John P. Bakewell, Pittsburg, for making furniture knobs.
up to 1830	Shearing-off marks on rims.
by 1830	Handles of vessels applied by fixing to body at base then looping up.
1827	Enoch Robinson and Deming Jarvis pressed hollow glass.
1830	John McGann, Philadelphia, issued patent for pressing bottles.
1830	Three-part mold in use.
1730 to 1830	Alkali from burned kelp imported into England from Scotland.
1830s to 1840s	Cake salt from first stage of LeBlanc's process increases use of sodium sulphate, which had diminished due to high cost of LeBlanc process's final product, sodium carbonate.
1830s to 1880s	Renaissance Revival styles.
1839	Verein zur Beförderung des Gewerbefleisses (Prussia) announces prize for discovery of Venetian technique for threaded glass. Won by Franz Pohl.
1840s to 1880s	Gothic and Greek revivals.
1840	Egermann discovers method to stain glass red. Not flashing.
	For silvering mirrors, chemical deposit of silver nitrate supplants amalgam of tin and mercury used since 1317.
	J. Crosfield discovers flame furnace, forerunner of tank furnace.
	Achilles Christian Wilhelm Friedrich von Faber der Faur discovers how to make gas and the gas generator. He was mining director to King of Württemberg.

1843	Large iron plates available for plate glass casting beds. Earlier beds made of copper, which split.
1850 to 1880	Era of expansion in use of gas for fuel and illumination.
1850-60	Bottle pontil disappears with introduction of snap case method.
1850s	Neo-rococo style in vogue.
1851	Great Exhibition, England.
	Rolled plate glass rejected for Crystal Palace in favor of Harley's lighter cylinder.
	Perry opens Japan to the West: negotiates first U.S.-Japanese treaty.
1856	Embossing on glass developed: C.D. Gardissal applies resist before hydrofloric acid acts on uncoated portion. Resist made of colophony and beeswax or elemi and Judaea bitumen.
1856	Siemens regenerative furnace is introduced.
1858	James Napier, England, develops method of printing decoration on glass. Design was drawn with printer's ink on paper, pasted on glass with ink next to glass, then etched with hydrofluoric acid.
	Bigland and Worral take out similar patent.
1859	Bottle blowing machine patented in England.
1860	Glass made with relief effects at Bigland & Worral, England.
	Samuel Clarke develops slow-burning safety candle.
1861	Northwood invents template machine.
	Metal stencil to decorate glass is developed by Charles Bishop.
	Strassfurt potash (potassium carbonate) deposits developed.
	First gas furnace installed in England.
	Solvay (Belgium) introduces manufacture of sodium carbonate by ammonia-soda process. Soda price falls and soda again becomes major source of alkali.

1862	London World Exhibition features display of Chinese Art.
	Exhibition of England's Japanese ambassador's collection of Japanese art. First time Japanese art seen in West.
1864	Crystal pattern glass decoration: F. Kuhlunn, Paris. Thick solution crystalizes on glass (clear or colored crystal). Then, acid etched.
	William Leighton, worker at Hobbs, Brockunier & Co., improves lime glass; substitutes bicarbonate of soda for poor grade soda ash, and perfects proportions. Lead (flint) is replaced for pressed glass.
1865-66	Chilled iron molds are introduced with smooth surfaces that eliminated need to fire polish bottles.
1865	Gillinder patents method to make pitchers by first pressing, then freehand blowing them.
1867	Second Paris World Exposition. Awakened interest in neo-Venetian glass due to Pohl's threading technique.
	Paris World Exposition: newly discovered art of Egypt seen.
1868	Eastlake's *Hints of Household Taste*, based on medieval and Jacobean designs published.
1869	Opening of Suez Canal.
1870s	Tops of chimneys decorated.
1870	Sandblasting first used by Benjamin Chew Tilghman. Patented in every country of world.
1871	Opera *Aïda* by Verdi first performed. Stimulated use of Egyptian themes.
1872	Lötz patents method to iridize glass.
1873	Exhibit by Lobmeyer of cut and engraved glass at Vienna World Exposition. Venetian style goes out, cut and engraved comes in.
1874	Thaddeus Hyat embosses plate glass while it is still soft on casting table.
1875 to 1890s	Moorish-mosque style.

1876	Hodgett introduces threading machine in England.
	C. Hollyer, London, creates light and shade effect on embossed plate glass by use of stencils.
1877	Parent company of Thomas Evans secures patent rights to crimping machine for piecrust edge.
1878	Swan introduces cucumber-shaped carbon filament lamp.
1879	Edison introduces pear-shaped lamp with bamboo filament.
by 1880	Twenty-one Siemens' regenerative-type gas furnaces in use in U.S.A.
1880	Cleopatra's "Needle" to New York City.
	Northwood invents herringbone machine.
after 1880	Hand-operated side lever press becomes obsolete.
1881	First house lighted by electricity.
	Tiffany patents method to trap air between two layers of glass.
1882	Tiffany makes fixtures for White House.
1883	George A. Macbeth patents "Pearl Top" chimney.
1884	Rochester burner introduced.
	Fritz Heckert patents method to blow glass into metal form.
1887	Northwood introduces intaglio cutting in England.
	F. Egermann introduces electrically driven polishing apparatus, perfected by Bohemian Kreybich at Reichswerk, Krasna.
	Joseph Locke patents method of applying a metallic stain to decorate glass. Applied wholly or in part, or used with volatile liquid that evaporated and left a mottled surface when fired in muffle furnace.
1888	First continuous tank furnace for window glass in use.
1890	B. Z. Meth and Kreitner etch glass with liquid by rubber stamp.

Cleopatra first performed with Sarah Bernhardt as leading actress.

1892   Tiffany introduces "Favrile" glass.

1893   Arbogast patents semi-automatic press-blow machine requiring operator to feed glass.

Introduction of Welsbach mantle by Carl von Welsbach.

Tiffany shows first leaded glass umbrella and dome shades at Chicago World's Fair.

1895-
1910   Art Nouveau movement.

1895   Bing opens gallery in Paris: Galleries de l'Art Nouveau.

Tiffany's first success with iridescent glass.

1898   W.J. Miller introduces fully automatic glass press (U.S.)

Tiffany's first public promotion of lamps.

1899   Tiffany patents "Nautilus" design.

Owens patents process for pressing and fire polishing blanks for tableware to be finished by skilled cutters. Used with "Rich Cut" glass.

Twentieth Century

by 1900   Strings used to eliminate gadget marks on foot of glass vessels (England).

Wooden foot clappers used to eliminate striation marks.

1900   Paris International Exposition. Tiffany shows "Lily" lamp for first time.

about
1900   Owens sells patent to Fry for pressed, fire-polished blanks.

1900   Window glass still only handmade.

early
1900s   Pantograph used for decorating goblets simultaneously by scratching design in coat of wax.

1902   Tiffany patents "Favrile" and introduces "drapery" glass.

1902-4   Emil Fourcault introduces vertical drawing of sheet glass in Belgium.

1903   Libbey adopts Owens's machine to press and fire-polish blanks for tablewares.

American Window Glass Co. introduces automatic cylinder machine developed by John Lubbers.

1906   Coburn process for drawn sheet glass is introduced.

1909   Neo-Greek and neo-Roman styles popular.

1910   Lubbers cylinder machine introduced into Britain.

McKee Glass Co. adopts Owens's blowing-polishing machine.

1912   Multiple mold machine for tumblers developed.

1914   Tiffany introduces "Damascene."

1915   All American window glass still made by cylinder method.

1916   Owens first to successfully apply continuous drawing to sheet glass, giving it a natural fire polish.

1917   Continuous automatic feeding machine developed that adds molten glass lumps of the correct size to mold.

First machine to make lightbulbs developed.

by 1920   Continuous lear annealing oven introduced.

Grinding and polishing automated.

Most glass furnaces in U.S. fueled by gas.

1910-
1920s   Adam Revival style popular.

1922-27   Acid polishing introduced by Wilkinson & Co., England.

1925   Wilkinson replaces horizontal steel cutting wheels with upright carborundum wheels.

King Tut's tomb opened in Egypt.

Exhibit des Art Decoratif, Paris, initiates the Art Deco movement.

1950s   Oil and gas furnace output boosted by 100 percent with electricity. Quality of glass improves.

Bibliography

American Glass Review. "Glass Factory Index." Feb. 28, 1976. (AGR)

Amic, Yolande. *L'Opaline Française au XIX Siècle.* Paris: Librairie Oründ, 1952.

Annuaire National du Verre. Paris: Office d'Etudes Publicitaires, 1970. (ANV)

Arwas, Victor. *Glass: Art Nouveau to Art Deco.* New York: Rizzoli, 1977.

Auila, George C. *The Pairpoint Glass Story.* New Bedford, Mass., 1968.

Beard, Geoffrey W. *Nineteenth Century Cameo Glass.* Newport, Monmouthshire, England: Ceramic Book Company, 1956.

Benezit, E. *Dictionnaire des Peintres, Sculpteurs, Dessinateurs et Graveurs.* Paris: Librairie Grund, 1976.

Bennett, Harold. *The Cambridge Glass Book.* No publisher.

Berlin Kunstgewerbemuseum, Barbara Mundt Collection. Berlin: Staatsliche Museum, 1973.

Berlin Staatsliche Museum Kunstgewerbemuseum Werke um 1900. Berlin, 1966. (BSMK)

Billeter, Erika Gysling. *Objects des Jugendstils.* Berlin: Benteli Verlag, 1969.

Bley, Alice. *A Guide to Fraudulent Lalique.* Pepper Pike, Ohio: 1981.

Bloch-Dermant, Janine. *Art of French Glass.* N.Y.: Vendome Press, 1974.

————. *Verre en France d'Emile Gallé à nos joure.* Les Editions de l'Amateur, 1983.

Blount, Berniece and Henry. *French Cameo Glass.* Des Moines: Wallace-Homestead Book Co., 1968.

Boggess, Gill and Louise. *American Brilliant Cut Glass.* N.Y.: Crown, 1977.

Bott, Gerhard. *Kunsthandwerk um 1900 Jundgendstill.* Darmstadt: Edvard Roether, 1965.

British Glass Industries. *Directory and Buyers Guide.* London: Thomas Skinner Ed., 1965. (DBG)

Brohan, Karl H. *Kunsthandwerk Samlung.* Brohan, 1976.

Charleston, Robert J. *Masterpieces of Glass: a World History.* New York: Abrams, 1980.

Cloak, Evelyn Campbell. *Glass Paperweights at the Bergstrom Art Center.* N.Y.: Bonanza Books, 1975.

Collector's Encyclopedia: Victoriana to Art Deco. N.Y.: Random House, 1974.

Cronin, J.R. *Fake and Forged Trade Marks on Old and New Glass.* Pueblo, Colo.: Grafika, 1976.

Darling, Sharon S. *Chicago Ceramics and Glass.* Chicago: Chicago Historical Society, 1979.

Daum et Cie. *One Hundred Years of Glass and Crystal.* Washington, D.C.: Daum et Cie and the Smithsonian, 1978.

Davis, Dereck C. *English Bottles and Decanters.* N.Y.: The World Print Co., 1972.

Duncan, Alastair. *Tiffany at Auction.* N.Y.: Rizzoli, 1981.

————. *Tiffany Windows.* N.Y.: Simon & Schuster, 1980.

Eville, E. M. *Paperweights and Other Glass Curiosities.* London: Spring Books, 1954.

European Glass Directory and Buyers Guide. London: Fuel and Metallurgical Journals, Ltd., 1975. (EGD)

Farrar, Estelle Sinclair and Spillman, Jane Shadel. *The Complete Cut and Engraved Glass of Corning.* N. Y.: Crown.

Fauster, Carl U. *Libbey Glass Since 1818.* Toledo, Ohio: Len Beach Press, 1979.

Florence, Gene. *Collectors Encyclopedia of Akro Agate Glassware.* Paducah, KY: Collectors Books, 1975.

Gardner, Paul V. *The Glass of Frederick Carder.* N.Y.: Crown, 1971.

Gardner, Phillippe. *Emile Gallé.* N.Y.: Rizolli, 1976.

Gessert, Dr. M. A. and Framberg, Emanuel, O. H. *The Art of Painting on Glass or Glass Staining.* London: Crosby Lockwood, 1884.

Gift and Tableware Reporter. (G&T)

Graham, Marjorie. *Australian Glass of the 19th and Early 20th Centuries.* Sidney: Davil Ell Press, 1981.

Grant, Joanne. *The Painted Lamps of Handel.* N.Y.: C. Cornwall-on-Hudson, 1978.

Grimmer, Elsa. *Wave Crest Ware: An Illustrated Guide to the Victorian World of C. F. Monroe.* Des Moines, Iowa: Wallace-Homestead Book Co., 1979.

Grover, Ray and Lee. *Art Glass Nouveau.* Rutland, Vt.: Tuttle, 1967.

———. *Carved and Decorated European Art Glass.* Rutland, Vt.: Tuttle, 1978.

———. *English Cameo Glass.* N.Y.: Crown, 1980.

Gysling-Billeter, Erika. *Objekte des Jugendstills.* Berlin: Benteli Verlag, 1969.

Hase, Ulrike von. *Schmuck in Deutschland und Osterreich 1895-1914.* Munich: Prestel, 1977.

Haslam, Malcom. *Marks and Monograms of the Modern Movement 1875-1930.* N.Y.: Scribners, 1977.

Heuser, Hans Jürgen and Co., *Hamburg Miscellanea.* Hamburg: Heuser Kunsthandler, n.d.

Hilschenz, Helga. *Das Glas des Jugendstill.* Düseldorf: Düseldorf Kunstmuseum, n.d.

Honey, William Bower. *Glass: A Handbook and Guide to the Museum Collection.* London: Victoria and Albert, 1948.

Innes, Lowell. *Pittsburgh Glass 1797-1891.* Boston: Houghton Mifflin, 1976.

Institute für neue technische form. Darmstadt Weisbaden: Staaten Verlag, 1962, n. 3.

Jokelson, Paul. *Sulphides.* N.Y.: Galahad Books, 1968.

Jubilaumsbedichte: Anlässich der 80 Jarhigen Bestandiges der Deutschen Staatsfachschule für Glasindustrie in Steinsschonau. Anstatt: Eigenverlag der Anstatt, 1936.

Jugendstil: Bearbeit von Irmela Franzke. Karlsruhe: Badisches Landesmuseum, 1978.

Klesse, Brigitte. *Glas vom Jugendstil bis Heute.* Köln: Walther König, 1981.

Körting, W. *Gläser und Getränke.* Bamberg: Meisenbach, 1967.

Kovel, Ralph and Terry. *Price Guide for Collector Plates, Figurines, Paperweights and Other Limited Editions.* N.Y.: Crown, 1974, 1978.

Kunsthandwerk im Umbruch Mosel. Hanover: Chridel, 1971.

Lagerberg, Ted and Vi. *Emil J. Larson and Durand Glass.* New Port Richey, Florida, n.d.

Leerdam Unica: 50 Jahre Modernes Neiderlandesches Glas. Düsseldorf: Düseldorf Kunstmuseum, 1977.

Manley, Cyril. *Decorative Victorian Glass.* London: Wark Lock, 1981.

McDonald, Ann Gilbert. "Milk Glass Lamps and the Northwood-Dugan Connection." *Antique Trader.* Feb. 27, 1985; p. 97.

McKean, Hugh F. *The Lost Treasures of Louis Comfort Tiffany.* N. Y.: Doubleday, 1980.

McKearin, George S. and Helen. *200 Years of American Blown Glass.* Garden City: Doubleday, 1950.

Meadows, Cecil A. *Discovering Oil Lamps.* London: Shire Publications, 1972.

Melvin, Jean S. *American Glass Paperweights and Their Makers.* Camden, N. J.: Thomas Nelson, Inc., 1970.

Messanelle, Ray. "Art Glass Signed Nash." *Spinning Wheel.* Feb. 1962, pp. 12-13.

Middlemans, Keith. *Continental Colored Glass.* London: Barrie and Jenkins, 1971.

Museum für Kunsthandwerk. *Modernes Glas Aus Amerika, Europe und Japan.* Frankfurt am Main: Museum für Kunsthandwerk, 1976. (MfK)

Neuwirth, Waltraud. *Das Glas des Jugendstills, Samlung des Osterreischen Museums für Angewandte Kunst.* Wien: Watraud, 1973.

Newman, Harold. *An Illustrated Dictionary of Glass.* London: Thames and Hudson, 1977.

Nový Bor Sttárske Museum Art Deco. Praque: Bižuterrie, 1980.

Official 1984 Price Guide to Glassware. Orlando, FL: House of Collectibles, 1984.

Padgett, Leonard E. *Pairpoint Glass.* Des Moines, Iowa: Wallace-Homestead Book Co., 1979.

Pazaurek, Gustav. *Gläser der Empire und Biedermeier Zeit. Kunstgläser der Gegenwart.* Leipzig: Klinkhardt und Biermann, vol. XIX/XX, 1925.

Pearson, J. Michael. *Encyclopedia of American Cut and Engraved Glass.* Miami Beach, FL: J. Michael Pearson, 1975.

Percy, Christopher Vane. *The Glass of Lalique, A Collector's Guide.* N.Y.: Charles Scribner's Sons, 1977.

Peterson, Arthur G. *400 Trademarks on Glass.* Arthur G. Peterson, 1968.

Polak, Ada. *Glass, Its Traditions.* N.Y.: Putnam, 1975.

_____. *Modern Glass*. N.Y.: Thomas Yoseloff, 1962.

_____. "Signatures on Gallé Glass." *Journal of Glass Studies*. Bd. 8, 1966.

Ptocku. *Museum Mozowieckie W. Potocku Katalog*. 1978.

Revi, Albert C. *Nineteenth Century Glass*. Camden, N.J.: Thomas Nelson, 1976.

_____. *American Cut and Engraved Glass*. N.Y.: Thomas Nelson and Sons, 1965.

Ricke, Helmut. *Glas de Art Deco*. Hanover: Kunst und Antiquitäten, 1981.

Roberts, Darrah L. *Art Glass Shades*. Des Moines: Wallace-Homestead Book Co., 1968.

_____. *Collecting Art Nouveau Shades*. Des Moines, Iowa: Wallace-Homestead, 1972.

Savage, George. *Glass of the World*. N.Y.: Galahad Books, n.d.

_____. *Dictionary of Nineteenth Century Antiques*. N.Y.: G. P. Putnam's Sons, 1978.

Schack, Clementine. *Ein Glaskunst ein Handbuch über Herstellung Samlung in Gegrauch des Hohlglases*. Munich: Keyseresch Verlag, 1976.

Schwandt, Jörg. *W M F Glas, Keramik, Metal*. Berlin: Kunstgewerke Museum Staatliche Museum Prussicher Kultur Besitz, 1980.

Schweiger, Werner J. *Wiener Werkstätte*. N.Y.: Abbeville Press, 1984.

St. Aubin. L.O. *Pairpoint Lamps*. Pine Tree Press, 1974.

Stevens, Gerald F. *Canadian Glass Circa 1825-1925*. Toronto: Reyerson, 1967.

Stout, Sandra McPhee. *The Complete Book of McKee Glass*. North Kansas City: Trojan Press, 1972.

Swan, Frank H. *Portland Glass*. Des Moines: Wallace-Homestead Book Co., n.d.

Trademarks of the Jewelry and Kindred Trades. N.Y.: Jewelers Circular Publishing Co., 1915.

Taub, Jules S. *The Glass of Désiré Christian*. San Francisco: Art Glass Exchange, 1978.

Uecker, Wolf. *Lamps and Candlesticks: Art Nouveau-Art Deco*. Herrsching: Schuler, 1978.

Unitt, Doris Joyce. *Unitt's Book of Marks: Antiques and Collectables*. Petersborough, Ontario: Clock House Publishers, 1973.

van der Meer, Singelanberg. *Nederlands Keramick en Glasmerken 1880-1940*. Lochem: de Tijdstroom, 1980.

Venzmer, Wolfgang. *Jugendstilsglas Samlung*. Mainz: H.R. Gruber, 1976.

Verrieres d'Art Lorriane. *Catalogue*. n.d.

Verrieres Signées D'Avesn: Price List. 1930.

Wakefield, Hubert George. *Nineteenth Century British Glass*. N.Y.: Yoseloff, 1962.

Weatherman, Hazel Marie. *Colored Glassware of the Depression Era*. Springfield, Mo.: Weatherman, 1970.

Weiss, Gustav. *The Book of Glass*. N.Y: Praeger, 1971.

Whitlow, Harry H. *Art, Colored and Cameo Glass*. Riverview, Mich.: 1960.

Wilkinson, R. *The Hallmarks of Antique Glass*. London: Richard Madley Ltd., 1968.

Wills, Goeffrey. *Victorian Glass*. London: G. Bell, 1976.

_____. *English and Irish Glass*. Garden City, N. Y.: Doubleday, 1968.

Wittenau, Clementine Schack. *Glas Zwischen Kunsthandwerk und Industriedesign*. Köln: Philosophical Dissertation, 1971.

Woeckel, Dr. Gerhard P. *Staatliche Kunstsammlungen*. Munchen/Kassel: 1968.

Index

About the Author

Anne Pullin is a full-time appraiser of decorative and fine arts in Orlando, Florida. She earned a senior membership in the American Society of Appraisers and also, after a thirty-hour written essay and a one-day oral examination, became a member of the Incorporated Society of Valuers and Auctioneers of London. She is listed in the first edition of *Who's Who and Why of Successful Florida Women*. She has spoken before national appraisal organizations and at seminars sponsored by museums.

The author's familiarity with art and antiques began in childhood when she was dragged to sales and shops by her collecting mother. She maintained a serious interest in art and earned a Bachelor of Fine Arts from Newcomb College in New Orleans. When asked how she acquired her knowledge of art and antiques, she replies that she spent hours studying while waiting at the pediatrician's office, at scout meetings, and at dance classes while her children were growing up.

She is currently working on a Master of Valuation Science degree through Hofstra University. This book is the by-product of a paper, "Art That Shades the Glare," which the author wrote for one of her projects. As an appraiser, Anne feels that she stands on a bridge between the retail trade and research fields, for she believes that evaluating aesthetics and historical position must be considered before market analysis begins.